Cambridge Elements

Elements in the History and Politics of Fascism
edited by
Federico Finchelstein
The New School for Social Research
António Costa Pinto
University of Lisbon

NEOFASCISM AND THE FAR RIGHT IN BRAZIL

Odilon Caldeira Neto
Federal University of Juiz de Fora

Shaftesbury Road, Cambridge, CB2 8EA, United Kingdom

One Liberty Plaza, 20th Floor, New York, NY 10006, USA

477 Williamstown Road, Port Melbourne, VIC 3207, Australia

314–321, 3rd Floor, Plot 3, Splendor Forum, Jasola District Centre, New Delhi – 110025, India

103 Penang Road, #05–06/07, Visioncrest Commercial, Singapore 238467

Cambridge University Press is part of Cambridge University Press & Assessment, a department of the University of Cambridge.

We share the University's mission to contribute to society through the pursuit of education, learning and research at the highest international levels of excellence.

www.cambridge.org
Information on this title: www.cambridge.org/9781009535496

DOI: 10.1017/9781009535472

When citing this work, please include a reference to the DOI 10.1017/9781009535472

First published 2025

A catalogue record for this publication is available from the British Library

ISBN 978-1-009-53549-6 Hardback
ISBN 978-1-009-53550-2 Paperback
ISSN 2977-0416 (online)
ISSN 2977-0408 (print)

Neofascism and the Far Right in Brazil

Elements in the History and Politics of Fascism

DOI: 10.1017/9781009535472
First published online: February 2025

Odilon Caldeira Neto
Federal University of Juiz de Fora

Author for correspondence: Odilon Caldeira Neto, odilon.caldeira@ufjf.br

Abstract: Is there a history of neofascism in Brazil? The purpose of this Element is to analyze neofascism as a late phenomenon to understand its impacts and its connections with the so-called new rights, the radical right, and Bolsonarism. For this purpose, the Element is separated into three sections addressing the formation of the first neofascist organizations after the Brazilian democratic transition, the development and articulation of a transnational network amidst a sharpening political crisis, and the emergence of a more complex and active Brazilian framework in the global extreme-right scenario in recent years. The main argument is that, despite being a late phenomenon, neofascism managed to articulate itself and have a political impact in Brazil, and therefore requires further investigation to understand its complexity and diversity.

Keywords: fascism, neofascism, extreme right, Brazil, far right

ISBNs: 9781009535496 (HB), 9781009535502 (PB), 9781009535472 (OC)
ISSNs: 2977-0416 (online), 2977-0408 (print)

Contents

1 Introduction

A country that supposedly has no right wing. That was how parts of the Brazilian political class saw the country in 1985, according to a survey of deputies participating in the Constituent Assembly, which was responsible for drafting a new constitutional charter that would mark the beginning of the Sixth (and "New") Brazilian Republic after the end of the civil–military dictatorship (1964–1985) (Rodrigues, 1987; Pierucci, 1987). After the transition to democracy, the hegemonic sectors of Brazilian society considered the issue of right-wing authoritarianism a thing of the past, limited to a few nostalgic military officers and radical civilians who insisted on rejecting the end of the dictatorship. But the following decades proved otherwise. The Brazilian far right survived and managed to rally and reinvent itself, building a rich, transnational network. This phenomenon affected even the most extreme corner of Brazilian right-wing movements: namely, neofascism.

The rights are now both a part of Brazilian history and a major element of daily political life. Since independence and the formation of a national identity, the right has been grouped into fascists, conservatives, authoritarians, liberals, traditionalists, Catholics, et cetera. In recent decades, new, more radical right-leaning groups and trends have emerged, a movement some studies have coined a "conservative wave" or "new right," among other terms.

In recent years, the election and presidential mandate of Jair Bolsonaro and its surrounding events have justifiably provoked growing concern in respect of this topic. After the end of the Bolsonaro government, a coup attempt on January 8, 2023 combined a set of actions inspired by international examples (e.g., the attack on the Capitol in Washington, DC), including patterns from the extensive history of the Brazilian far right. Thus, to understand the Brazilian context, one must explore aspects such as transnational circulation without ignoring the local and regional factors that influence this process. This integration between the global/international and the local/regional greatly helped in leveraging the extreme-right agendas in Brazil, as well as facilitating their reception.

This Element is grounded on the perspective that fascism is one of the most important points for comprehending the historical and current situation of Brazilian right wings, based on an analysis of Brazilian neofascism and its interactions with a part of the political field: the far right (Pirro, 2022; Mudde, 2019).

The importance of analyzing fascism arises from its historical framework and reverberations. The Brazilian Integralist Action, founded in 1932, was the main fascist organization outside Europe and had a strong presence in the Brazilian political, religious, and military sectors. In fact, it was the first mass political organization in the country, even before entities such as the Brazilian Communist Party. Moreover, in addition to the institutional articulation and its green shirts and blouses, fascist groups and trends have enormously contributed to the amalgam that is the Brazilian – and even Latin American – political right-wing culture, centered around a radical political stance based on issues such as anticommunism and Catholicism (Boisard, 2014), as well as the defense of authoritarian values and regimes.

The analysis framework I use in this Element considers fascism as a global phenomenon – that is, not exclusively European nor restricted solely to the interwar period. By following this analytical and interpretative framework, I argue that fascisms developed autonomous trajectories outside Europe, particularly in Latin America (Finchelstein, 2019), establishing relations with the armed forces, the Catholic Church, and intellectuals and authoritarian regimes with a corporatist approach (Costa Pinto, 2019). This history did not end after the "era of fascism," and we can now effectively speak about a history of neofascism, with its new characteristics and political processes (Copsey, 2020). By extension, neofascism encompasses a wide-ranging universe of organizations, groups, intellectuals, and political initiatives that seek to recapture fundamental aspects of the organizations and/or core ideas of twentieth-century fascist movements.

The history of neofascism in Brazil developed at a different pace compared to countries such as Italy and France. Contrary to a certain "synchronicity" between fascisms in the first half of the twentieth century, the post-1945 context brought new challenges. In Latin America, some of the fascists adapted to the "postfascist" context, integrating themselves into authoritarian regimes such as Peronism in Argentina or the Brazilian New State (Estado Novo) lead by Getúlio Vargas. In Western Europe, with a few exceptions such as the Iberian Peninsula, the post-fascist backdrop helped drive the first and second waves of the radical right. An essential turning (and starting) point for these waves was their departure from the "fascist condition" and the turn to radical right-wing populism (Von Beyme, 1988), in which the democratic condition became an imperative for political groups once associated with fascism and authoritarianism.

Being publicly associated with fascism was an issue due to the political and electoral risk it imposed. That was an immediate and common condition that fascist groups shared on both continents. However, after the initial postwar years, there was a distinction between political frameworks, especially from the 1960s onward. While a significant part of Western Europe was fully involved in a broad process of consolidating liberal democracy as a governmental benchmark, Latin America would undergo a new authoritarian wave in the form of military dictatorships, which lasted until the 1980s. That is a highly important contextual element. It raises the following questions: How did neofascism develop in Brazil? And what is the impact of neofascism on the most recent rise of the far right in this country of undeniable regional importance? These questions are what I seek to answer in this Element.

I consider that the existence of an authoritarian wave in Latin America from the 1960s onward was one of the fundamental factors for neofascism to have an effective presence in Brazil only after the democratic transition, which can be called a "late phenomenon," especially compared to the European continent. The authoritarian structures, which provided few possibilities for insertion into political society, as well as the few ways of mobilizing political life, were factors that made it impossible for neofascist groups to integrate into the regime. In addition, the context of the 1960s and the demands of the Cold War (and the discourses in defense of democratic freedom) provided a kind of impediment to the usual rhetoric derived from the neofascist camp. That brings about some fundamental implications, which can be divided into two main issues.

The first is the relationship of neofascism to a broader local political framework. Although it might seem paradoxical, neofascism had some opportunities during the democratic transition as it sought to become more autonomous regarding its actions and organization. In subsequent years, this autonomy made it more ambitious in the democratic political game, as some neofascist tendencies got closer to or integrated with radical-right political parties.

In other words, neofascism was not (nor is currently) a major political player, but rather is a recurring presence in the radical political scene, especially from the twenty-first century onward. This type of political capital would later be important in moments of political crisis, such as the process that culminated in the impeachment of Dilma Rousseff of the Workers' Party (Partido dos Trabalhadores, PT), and particularly in the development of Bolsonarism, as well as during the moments of crisis and the later part of Bolsonaro's government.

The second implication concerns the strategies that Brazilian neofascism employed to be incorporated into a broader framework of international neofascism. Regarding the European extreme right, after the "revivalism" phase neofascist organizations moved away from the institutional arena and articulated themselves based on strategies such as deterritorialization and European internationalization (Mammone, 2001), revisionism and Holocaust denialism, and metapolitics (Copsey, 2020).

This neofascist groupuscular right (Griffin, 2003), inspired by the ethnodifferentialist agendas of the Nouvelle Droite and similar movements, intensified continental cooperation based on a pan-national, Europeanist agenda. This approach was immediately considered alien and inaccessible to the Brazilian context, not only due to its late rise but also because its identity agenda was dissociated from that of European neofascism. This is one factor that partially explains the most recent rise in internationalization seen in Brazilian neofascism. In short, neofascism is a late phenomenon in Brazil compared to Western Europe, and its capacity for internationalization results from an even more recent development: the impact of new technologies and the emergence of new groups in the Brazilian neofascist environment.

From this perspective, this work analyzes the history of neofascism in Brazil and its relationship with the Brazilian far right. The Element consists of three parts. The first section, "The First Neo-Fascist Wave (1980–2000)," provides an analysis of the birth of neofascism and its three main branches: neo-integralism, neo-Nazism, and Holocaust denialism. The second section, "The Second Neo-Fascist Wave (2000–2020)," presents the new forms of Brazilian neofascism, its initial internationalization process based on the incorporation of new strategies (such as metapolitics and identitarianism), and the search for new transnational spaces (such as the Fourth Political Theory), among others. The third section, "Dialogues between Neofascism and the Brazilian Far Right,"is a discussion of the Brazilian far right and how it interacts with neofascist groups, with an investigation of the strategies neofascist groups adopted during the most recent rise of the Brazilian radical right and the formation of Bolsonarism as a field of radical politics, as well as the impact of Bolsonarism on the neofascist camp. Finally, the conclusion points toward the new challenges that must be overcome to understand this constant and changing phenomenon in Brazilian radical politics.

2 The First Neofascist Wave (1980–2000)

2.1 The Origins of Fascism and Neofascism in Brazil

The impact of the "era of fascism" on the largest country in Latin America was evident. Inspired by European fascist movements and regimes and influenced by corporatism, anticommunism, and antiliberal discourses, Brazil's fascism started developing between the 1920s and 1930s. Some small organizations, such as the Brazilian Social Action (Ação Social Brasileira) group and the Ceará Legion of Labor (Legião Cearense do Trabalho), were the first fascist expressions in the country. In addition to grassroots groups, some parts of (notably German and Italian) immigrant communities were enthusiasts of the National Fascist Party or the Nazi Party (Bertonha & Athaídes, 2023). However, these initiatives were restricted to those immigrant spaces.

The Brazilian fascist scenario lacked a nation-encompassing entity that considered the country's specificities, a gap filled in 1932 when Brazilian Integralist Action (AIB) was founded. This institution was the flagship of integralism and consolidated itself as the primary fascist reference in Brazil and outside Europe. Wearing green shirts and blouses, the integralists formed an intensely bureaucratic, authoritarian, and paramilitary structure aimed at emulating what would later be a corporate totalitarian state inspired by the Italian experience (i.e., the Integral State).

Between 1932 and 1937, the AIB – led by the journalist and writer Plínio Salgado, alongside the intellectuals Gustavo Barroso and Miguel Reale – brought together hundreds of thousands of activists in a country with continental dimensions. Integralism was one of the main vectors for the spread of anticommunism, anti-Semitism, and antiliberalism in Brazil, and thus quickly consolidated itself as a mass political organization with strong representation among the urban middle classes, capable of establishing dialogues with sectors of the armed forces (especially the Navy) and strands of conservative Catholicism. Despite not assuming power, integralism was a critical ideological vector of fascism and a training ground for prominent political activists in subsequent decades.

In 1937, integralists supported the coup that led to the onset of the dictatorship – that is, the authoritarian New State (Estado Novo) of Getúlio Vargas – by helping spread anticommunist and anti-Semitic conspiracy theories (the Cohen Plan). Although some integralists joined the authoritarian regime, a significant part of the activists and ideologues sought to build a more radical alternative that culminated in a coup attempt. In March of 1938, the integralists were deemed politically illegal after a further failed coup.

The integralist leader was arrested and subsequently exiled to Portugal, where he stayed until the end of the Second World War (Gonçalves, 2014). During this period, he grew closer to the Portuguese New State and tried to adapt to his new surroundings and influences, such as Salazarism and Portuguese Christian democracy (Gonçalves & Caldeira Neto, 2022). When Salgado returned to Brazil (1946), he took over the People's Representation Party (Partido de Representação Popular), the main integralist entity in the postwar period.

The integralist/fascist allegiance was not a consensus inside the party but rather a contended subject among the base-level activists and the upper echelons of the hierarchy. At first, the party joined the anticommunist discourse of the Cold War, but without assuming a proper neofascist tone. At times, the party organized events that celebrated the fascist past (using the Sigma [i.e., the AIB symbol], public demonstrations with green shirts, etc.). However, these clashed with the "defascistization" discourse that the integralist leadership advocated.

Throughout the 1950s and 1960s, the main agents of right-wing radicalization in Brazil were parts of the military and some areas of organized civil society that were calling for a coup. The fascist alternative did not gain prominence, so it was up to the integralists to articulate themselves as secondary participants in major public demonstrations – the "Marches of the Family with God for Liberty" – which helped mobilize the movement that culminated in the 1964 coup. With the beginning of the civil–military dictatorship, the process of political curtailment gained power, leading to the end of multipartisanship and the closure of all political parties, including the Integralist Party.

The bipartisanship established in 1966 based on the legal framework of the military regime (Napolitano, 2018) led to the creation of the National Renewal Alliance (Aliança Renovadora Nacional) party, bringing together several right-wing movements that supported the coup, including the integralists. However, during the dictatorship, the right-wing party was never markedly integralist, and the former leader of the Green Shirts was a politically irrelevant figure from the perspective of the majority. Still, Salgado was the undisputed leader of the Brazilian fascists. The creator of integralism was a synthesis of ideology, leadership, and activism – in short, a typical fascist leader in a postfascist era.

Salgado died in 1975, and the integralists lost their political figurehead and were left with no representatives who could immediately articulate the movement amidst the national neofascist camp. It must be taken into account that, during the 1970s and 1980s, the Brazilian political scenario was undergoing a slow process of political opening supervised by the military, which involved issues such as amnesty for military personnel, including torturers, and standstills and obstacles around topics such as transitional justice and politics of memory.

Even so, small non-neofascist extreme right-wing groups – such as the Anticommunist Movement (Movimento Anti Comunista) and the Communist Hunting Commando (Comando de Caça aos Comunistas) – came together in reaction to the democratic transition, using bomb attacks as a radicalization strategy (Farias, 2023).

Some military circles were pressuring the democratization movement, characterized by internal tendencies in the armed forces (Chirio, 2018) and the creation of pressure groups and military right-wing press vehicles, such as the newspapers *Ombro a Ombro* (*Shoulder to Shoulder*), *Letras em Marcha* (*Marching Letters*), and so forth. In fact, this was when the figure of Bolsonaro emerged as a political leader among low-ranking military personnel (Santos, 2022).

It was a time when integralism had to reinvent itself. Without Salgado, there were disputes over his political legacy: arguing over distinct interpretations of integralist ideology, discussing how to organize themselves, and even competing for potential leadership roles, a defining aspect of neo-integralism (Caldeira Neto, 2019). However, in addition to its impact on the roots of neo-integralism, the transition process toward democracy enabled the articulation of new trends that converged into the same neofascist universe (e.g., denialists, neo-Nazi groups, and White Power skinheads).

Although seemingly paradoxical, it was precisely at this moment of transition toward democracy that neofascism gained the space and autonomy it needed to develop. With the departure of the military from the scene and their extreme-right sectors ostracized, there was more room for other groups that converged around the defense of authoritarian, antidemocratic, anti-Semitic, and antiliberal values to articulate and claim political identities associated with twentieth-century fascist experiences. Thus, in Brazil, neofascism developed in distinct phases when compared to the European phenomenon (Bull, 2012). The first phase of Brazilian neofascism developed a three-part framework consisting of neo-integralism, Holocaust denialism and neo-Nazi tendencies.

2.2 Neo-Integralism

In general terms, neo-integralism can be defined as those groups, people, and organizations that claimed to be integralists after the death of Salgado. His death left a gap in the power structures, but also enabled neo-integralist groups to develop new dynamics influenced by a shared repertoire from transnational spaces.

That immediately created a problematic environment, not only from a political and pragmatic perspective but also in dealing with the memories of the movement. After 1975, a share of the integralists argued in favor of integralism having noninstitutional actions, seeking to build spaces and celebrate the remembrance of the moment, in addition to occasionally holding meetings to discuss the integralist doctrine. Another, more active segment of the activists expressed the need for more concrete, even institutional, integralist action. That led to an initial rupture within neo-integralism. Some neo-integralists even advocated creating a political party following the abolition of bipartisanship in 1979.

The years immediately after Salgado's death were marked by the almost complete absence of integralist movement and organizations, or else by the ephemeral nature of some of them, such as the Popular Movement in Support of the Plínio Salgado Foundation (Movimento Popular de Apoio à Fundação Plínio Salgado) and the National Renewal Crusade (Cruzada de Renovação Nacional), an entity that sought to participate in the debates around the democratic transition but that was disrupted by the remaining integralists themselves.

In fact, the first impactful neo-integralist organization was Casa Plínio Salgado, which opened in 1981 in the city of São Paulo (Carneiro, 2012).

With its own archive and library, Casa Plínio Salgado had the purpose of celebrating the memories of the movement, but it also acted as a meeting point where old and new activists could express themselves politically. This memorialistic integralist space enabled a social network to be established around shared interests and political endeavors. Among the various acronyms that emerged from this remembrance of integralism, the one that played a central role from the perspective of neo-integralist political institutionalization was the project to recreate the Brazilian Integralist Action (AIB).

This Brazilian Integralist Action, founded in 1985, was assembled in particular by Anésio de Lara Campos Junior, a second-generation integralist (from the People's Representation Party). Although he was an active member of integralist movements even before Salgado's death, Anésio Lara was not recognized as the undisputed leader of neo-integralism, for several reasons. A significant factor was the lack of approval from Salgado's direct heirs, his family members, and his closest integralists. These "heirs" were averse to – or openly opposed – any political initiatives by integralism or integralists, at least from an institutionalized perspective. Therefore, the proposal to reestablish the AIB stirred the neo-integralist field.

For some integralists, although the acronym AIB was available for registration (as it had been dissolved after the New State coup in 1937), the nonconsensual registration could be interpreted as Anésio Lara and his companions somewhat "usurping" the memory of integralism. And, beyond the disputes among those who saw themselves as authentic heirs of Salgado regarding the memory of Plínio's political and symbolic capital and how politically institutional it should be, neo-integralism was divided between activists who planned a formal institutional path (i.e., a political party) or a tendency to adopt a more memorialist tone.

One of the first neo-integralist organizations that envisaged the possibility of partisan action was the Brazilian Nationalist Action (Ação Nacionalista Brasileira), created in 1985. Despite its fleeting nature, it signaled the effective beginning of a political reassembly process. Other integralists sought to engage in political party projects, such as the Nationalist Action Party (Partido de Ação Nacionalista), led by lawyer Rômulo Augusto Romero Fontes and financed by the Brazilian Cause Church (Igreja Causa-Brasil), described as the political-ideological and operational branch of the so-called Moon Cult (Dreifuss, 1989). In 1989, there was another attempt to articulate a neo-integralist party. Some integralists sought to create the Integralist Action Party (Partido de Ação Integralista), which included neo-integralist leaders such as the lawyer Jader Medeiros, who had been the leader of the National Renewal Crusade, the first effectively neo-integralist group.

But, in fact, Anésio Lara's AIB marked the first stage of a neo-integralist organization. Seeking to abstract the discussion surrounding political parties, this "second AIB" built an effective relationship with urban youth groups and subcultures brewing in the city of São Paulo.

In the 1980s, one of the urban youth cultures that emerged was the first Brazilian skinhead group, the Carecas do Subúrbio, or Shaved Heads from the Suburbs (Costa, 2000). These groups had characteristics similar to those of English skinhead groups: for example, low socioeconomic level and originating from industrial areas, as well as aesthetic, cultural, and behavioral elements (clothing, symbols, music, etc.).

The Carecas do Subúrbio had a diffuse political identity based on values such as nationalism and patriotism, male unity and fraternity, and a working-class facet based on manual and factory work – reference points for a collective identity that could be interpreted as a conservative perspective on customs, something that would later pave the way for this group to find similarities with the right wing. The Carecas gathered in the metropolitan area of the city of São Paulo, which was also a privileged place of activity for the first neo-integralist groups. At its beginning, the Carecas had a friendly relationship with groups from different ideologies, be that for their territorial proximity (from the same neighborhood, for example), shared musical tastes (Oi! music and punk rock bands), or, mainly, due to the historical origin of this seminal skinhead group, which emerged as an unfolding of Brazilian punk tendencies.

However, as this identity grew stronger, these groups were able to adopt increasingly intense sexist, authoritarian, and ultranationalist discourses. Encouraged and inspired by international tendencies that saw this gang as a fraternity that leaned on a more extremist and aggressive nationalism, these characteristics started being considered as core features of this Brazilian group, even compared to other youth styles, especially the punks. Despite their shared common roots, the Carecas became a right-wing/patriotic style, while the punks leaned toward the left/anarchism. At this moment, Anésio Lara and the AIB approached the Carecas, who were seen as potential active members of a paramilitarized youth for this new phase of integralism.

The fact that the Carecas accepted black people in their groups was a factor that garnered attention from the neo-integralist groups, which advocated that "racial democracy" should be a shared element of the Brazilian identity ethos. In any case, this had repercussions in the national press, creating discomfort in some sectors of the neo-integralist scene, as some groups opted for a less radical discourse and strategy, avoiding any direct association with groups routinely involved in the news regarding physical violence and attacks against minorities such as homosexuals, Jews, and migrants from the north and northeast of Brazil.

In addition to its relationship with skinheads, Anésio Lara's AIB got closer to other emerging Brazilian neofascist tendencies, such as neo-Nazism and Holocaust denialism. Anésio Lara himself became a known Holocaust denier, attacking Jewish entities and those who defended the memories surrounding the Holocaust. These issues, associated with the supposed "usurpation" of the acronym, meant that Anésio Lara's group was illegitimate, further intensifying the already disputed field of neo-integralism.

Between the 1980s and 1990s, neo-integralism remained a mere celebration of the movement's memory. In addition to Casa Plínio Salgado, the Plínio Salgado Culture Center was founded in the state of Rio de Janeiro, where it served as a physical meeting place and event space on important dates. However, in a country of continental dimensions, neo-integralism lacked a network that enabled the remaining integralists or even those who leaned toward international neofascism to establish broader relationships.

The neo-integralist scenario only changed from the 2000s onward, with the arrival and mild popularization of the internet in Brazil. The Integralist Studies and Debate Center (Centro de Estudos e Debates Integralistas, CEDI) was created amidst mailing lists, debate forums, and small websites run by young adults and teenagers, inaugurating the striking and articulated presence of neo-integralists in the digital space. Led by young student Marcelo Mendez, the CEDI was a neo-integralist initiative that abstained from establishing relationships with more extreme (neofascist) groups while trying to articulate with Catholic traditionalism.

Their alternative was to sever ties with the skinheads/Carecas and Holocaust denialists while strengthening their bonds with the Brazilian Society in Defense of Tradition, Family, and Property (TFP), an ultramontane Catholic entity founded by Plínio Correa de Oliveira in 1960. By focusing on a more Catholic discourse, they intended to hinder the presence of extreme groups that could potentially harm Marcelo Mendez's political purposes.

That was in vain, since the clashes between neo-integralist groups with different leanings intensified, culminating in the tragic suicide of Marcelo Mendez, which was motivated precisely by internal disputes. The neo-integralist scene collapsed, and an attempt at reconciliation only came to fruition in 2005, when neo-integralist groups and leaders organized the "First Integralist Congress of the 21st Century." The event was supposed to mark the creation of a unified integralist entity, but ended up marking the formation of three groups: the Revolutionary Integralist Action (Ação Integralista Revolucionária), the Brazilian Integralist and Linearist Movement (Movimento Integralista e Linearista Brasileiro), and the Brazilian Integralist Front (Frente Integralista Brasileira), which has been the most important neo-integralist organization since then.

Overall, this galaxy of neo-integralist groups shares fundamental values, such as the "cult" of their three leaders (Salgado, Gustavo Barroso, Miguel Reale) and the defense of an authoritarian fascist dictatorship with a corporatist approach. There are divergences regarding the interpretation of the integralist doctrine (some groups are more Catholic, others are markedly anti-Semitic), as well as in the relationship with the political universe as a whole (political parties, extreme-right groups, etc.).

Fragmentation aside, integralism has always been a fundamental reference for the Brazilian extreme right. Over their various generations, the integralists have successively adopted a discourse based on the traditional values of making society more Christian and moral, as well as a discourse grounded on the myth of racial democracy, despite their anti-Semitic traits and group identity based on a white, Christian model (on top of their project for a national identity with the characteristics).

This integralist political model enabled the establishment of dialogue with different political forces (such as conservatives, monarchists, Catholic traditionalists, military personnel, etc.), and this was precisely the kind of political capital that neo-integralist groups sought. Thus, neo-integralism was built as a "continuist" group that adapted to the demands of an authoritarian political culture ingrained in Brazilian society. Unlike some neo-integralists who sought to bring back and update integralism for the twentieth century, others who were articulating themselves in the same neofascist space brought with them more radical agendas that were absent from everyday Brazilian politics until that moment, such as Holocaust denialism and various neo-Nazi tendencies.

2.3 Holocaust Denialism

In Brazil, denialism as a phenomenon took shape simultaneously with the democratic transition and had an immediate political impact not only through its works and arguments but also because of the discussions surrounding the ban on denialist books after the censorship and amidst the calls for freedom of speech in the postdictatorship period.

The first references to denialism in the Brazilian public debate date back to the end of the 1970s. From 1977 onward, national newspapers such as *O Globo*, *Jornal do Brasil*, and *Folha de S. Paulo* covered the debate around the launch of David Irving's book *Hitler's War*, which marks Irving's support of denialism. Despite the international nature of the topic, the debate on it was influenced by the pressures surrounding the democratic transition, the limits of freedom of speech, and the publishing market against the backdrop of democracy.

In Brazil, the first structured denialist activities effectively happened after the consolidation of the "New Republic." The first and most famous denialist book by a Brazilian author was published in 1987: *Holocaust: Jewish or German? I Denounce: The Lie of the Century*, by Siegfried Castan Ellwanger, a Brazilian of German descent who signed his books with the pseudonym "S.E. Castan," supposedly to escape "Zionist persecution."

After the first book's release, Ellwanger founded the publishing house Revisão Editora, based in Porto Alegre, Rio Grande do Sul, to help spread the book and act as a denialist hub. For this purpose, Revisão had the explicit strategy of influencing the public debate by approaching the topic from a denialist perspective and disseminating an extensive anti-Semitic, denialist bibliography linked to neofascism.

Brazilian authors were a minority at Revisão Editora compared to the array of foreign, translated works. This bibliography consisted of books by denialists and/or anti-Semites such as Robert Faurisson, Roger Garaudy, Fred Leutcher Jr., and Louis Marschalko, among others. Most of the Brazilian works were written by Siegfried Ellwanger himself, followed by Sérgio Oliveira, a former Brazilian Army lieutenant who worked during the military dictatorship. There were also publications by lawyer and retired military officer Marco Polo Giordani, who defended Ellwanger in some of the lawsuits filed against him and Revisão Editora. Unlike Castan and Oliveira, Giordani gained prominence predominantly as a denier of the Brazilian dictatorship, not of events connected to the Holocaust.

To a large extent, works such as *Holocaust: Jewish or German? I Denounce: The Lie of the Century*, *SOS para Alemanha* (*SOS for Germany*), and *Acabou o Gás! . . . o fim de um mito* (*Out of Fuel! . . . The End of a Myth*) by Siegfried Ellwanger, as well as *Hitler: Culpado ou inocente?* (*Hitler: Guilty or Innocent?*) and *Sionismo x Revisionismo: Fantasia x Realidade* (*Zionism x Revisionism: Fantasy x Reality*) by Sérgio Oliveira, reproduced the bulk of international denialist arguments – that is, the emphasis on disqualifying the materiality and intentionality of the Holocaust, the outing of a supposed global Jewish articulation to manipulate global public opinion, and the alleged declaration of war by the Jews on Germany that (in their view) justified the genocide.

After the publication of *Holocaust: Jewish or German? I Denounce: The Lie of the Century* and an aggressive strategy to spread the news about the book, there was an extensive legal battle that encompassed several jurisdictions and lasted until 2003 when the case reached the Brazilian Supreme Court. The primary opponents of Revisão Editora and denialism in Brazil were human rights groups and Jewish entities that aimed to combat anti-Semitism and protect the memory of millions of Holocaust victims.

At first, there were boycotts to try to stop the spread of denialism, as opposing groups feared that filing a lawsuit would help publicize the topic and be used as justification for a victimization strategy. However, those opposing groups understood that the boycott was a one-off and did not bring substantial long-term results. Thus, some entities chose to pursue legal action.

This long dispute began in the Rio Grande do Sul courts. The first lawsuits against Revisão Editora were filed by the following entities: the Justice and Human Rights Movement (Movimento de Justiça e Direitos Humanos), the Porto Alegre Black Movement (Movimento Negro de Porto Alegre), and the Popular Anti-Racism Movement (Movimento Popular Anti Racismo). In 1995, Deputy Judge Bernadete Coutinho Friedrich deemed Siegfried Ellwanger innocent of the anti-Semitism and racism accusations brought by the Public Prosecutors Office. In her understanding, despite their content, Revisão Editora had the right to disseminate the books on the grounds of freedom of speech.

That caused a stir in various social groups, and there was much discussion about Bernadete Friedrich's capacity to judge the case, precisely because she was not the official holder of the position. After this episode, Jewish entities joined the legal battle against denialism. On December 27, 1995, the Israeli Federation of Rio Grande do Sul filed an appeal against the deputy judge's decision.

After an appeal filed by the Israeli Federation of Rio Grande do Sul and the mobilization of various parts of society, Ellwanger was found guilty and sentenced to two years in prison. The jury ruled out imprisonment of the denialist for fear that such action would give rise to a political martyrdom based on freedom of speech. As such, Ellwanger had his prison sentence revoked, and instead had to do community service for one year. Even so, Ellwanger and his lawyer requested habeas corpus before the Brazilian Supreme Court of Justice (Supremo Tribunal de Justiça, STJ), which garnered nationwide coverage of the case.

On December 18, 2001, the Brazilian Supreme Court of Justice denied the request filed by Ellwanger's attorney based on their understanding that the author had indeed committed a crime of racism. It should be emphasized that this lawsuit encompassed two complementary elements – the denialist works authored by Siegfried Ellwanger, and his role as one of the partners who owned Revisão Editora and used it to distribute the following anti-Semitic (some of them also denialist) books: *The International Jew*, by Henry Ford; *A História Secreta do Brasil* (*The Secret History of Brazil*), by Gustavo Barroso; *The Protocols of the Elders of Zion*, commented by Gustavo Barroso; *Brasil, Colônia de Banqueiros* (*Brazil, Colony of Bankers*), by Gustavo Barroso; *Hitler: Culpado ou inocente?* (*Hitler: Guilty or Innocent?*), by Sérgio Oliveira; and *The World Conquerors: The Real War Criminals*, by Louis Marschalko.

After Ellwanger's defeat before the Brazilian Supreme Court of Justice, his defense filed a request for habeas corpus, this time at the highest Brazilian jurisdiction, the Brazilian Federal Supreme Court (Supremo Tribunal Federal, STF). Under request number 82.4244, that process was widely publicized by the Brazilian press. Meanwhile, a series of protests led by Jewish entities and groups rose in defense of human rights due to the votes of some STF ministers who considered denialism a legitimate historiographical practice.

In practical terms, the request for habeas corpus filed by Ellwanger's attorney was an attempt to replace the accusation of racism with "discriminatory practices" to dismantle the argumentation. On September 17, 2003, the STF reached the final decision, and the request was denied by a (nonabsolute) majority of ministers. Ellwanger's sentence was maintained but converted to two years of community service.

As for books, the ban on the works and other activities of Revisão Editora was kept. However, that was not the end of denialism. Denialist groups started employing different strategies, such as donating works to universities and public libraries, converting them to digital format, and uploading the files to anti-Semitic websites and discussion forums, as well as selling copies in used book stores, even abroad.

Given that denialism was a topic that was not restricted to the Brazilian borders, there was an immediate integration between the most prominent authors of Revisão Editora and the international denialist market. Denialist books were sold using unconventional methods, such as via fax (based on promotional print material) and postal reimbursement, even amidst those legal disputes and after. From the 2000s onwards, the Revisão Editora website became a tool to spread texts and books edited or sold by the publisher.

These materials included a list of works by Brazilian denialist authors, nondenialist but anti-Semitic titles (such as *The International Jew* by Henry Ford and *The Secret Powers Behind Revolution* by León de Poncins), and foreign denialist works, such as those by Robert Faurisson (*Is the Diary of Anne Frank Genuine?*), C. W. Porter (*Not Guilty At Nuremberg: the German Defense Case*), and Richard Harwood (*Did Six Million Really Die?*).

Combined with this incursion into the field of transnational denialist authors, Revisão Editora translated Siegfried Ellwanger's books. *Holocaust: Jewish or German? I Denounce: The Lie of the Century*, for example, was translated into English, Spanish, and German. The translation effort and the legal disputes provided valuable political leverage for Revisão Editora while also enabling it to enter the international field of Holocaust denialism by building connections with the L'Association des Anciens Amateurs de Récits de Guerres et d'Holocaustes (AAARGH), founded in 1996.

The AAARGH was a denialist project that originally published material exclusively in French. In addition to disseminating denialist texts, it had archives dedicated to Robert Faurisson and Paul Rassinier, two of the most prominent French denialists, as well as works supporting other denialists, such as Roger Garaudy. From 2005 onwards, AAARGH began publishing a quarterly "historical criticism" newsletter in Portuguese titled *O Revisionismo em Língua Português* (*Revisionism in Portuguese*; curiously, the original title includes a gender agreement error; to comply with standard grammar rules, "Português" should be changed to "Portuguesa") and the motto "Não acredite. Pense" ("Don't believe. Think"). The newsletter was based on the works of both denialist authors and their critics, aiming for an impartial tone that was more aligned with the plurality of democracy.

Siegfried Ellwanger wrote some texts in a few editions (n. 1, n. 3, n. 5), but the Revisão Editora lawsuit was addressed on other occasions, up until the last edition of the newsletter (n. 8, 2008). The Portuguese version of AAARGH's main website listed some denialist works by Siegfried Ellwanger and Sérgio Oliveira.

In addition to references to the Revisão Editora, the AAARGH website had links to the "Inacredável" portal, which functioned as a spokesperson and a space for Brazilian denialists to gather virtually. Among the books from Revisão Editora available for download in PDF format, some of them had marks that signaled how these works were converted to a digital format and how they had circulated on the transnational field of denialism. The visual identities showcased on the digital versions of the files indicate that the website Valhalla88 (which presents itself as "the largest national socialist portal in South America on the Internet") was responsible for sharing *Acabou o Gás!* (Ellwanger); *Holocaust: Jewish or German? I Denounce: The Lie of the Century* (Ellwanger) and *O massacre de Katyn* (by Sérgio Oliveira), on the other hand, had the signs of Nuevo Ordem, a Spanish neofascist (and denialist) portal.

The Brazilian denialist movement thus found validation via its international counterparts. The website of Libreria Europa – a bookstore and publisher maintained by Spanish denialist Pedro Varela – included a list of references to denialist pages in other languages. The Revisão Editora website and its motto "Conferindo e divulgando a História" (Checking and disseminating history), were featured alongside the denialist *Journal of Historical Review*, which has ties to the Institute for Historical Review, as well as the German denialist website *Ernst Zündel*. It is essential to highlight that Pedro Varela, like Ellwanger, Zündel, and other authors in the field, became involved in lawsuits due to Holocaust denialism. Therefore, this affinity was not solely based on ideology, but was also a joint defense strategy.

This recognition by international denialists was something Siegfried Ellwanger longed for. Inspired by international initiatives, Revisão Editora sought to create denialist institutional bodies, like the National Center for Historical Research (Centro Nacional de Pesquisas Históricas, CNPH), founded in 1992 and clearly inspired by the North American model. The center was, in fact, a mere internal self-adulation body of Revisão Editora and its authors, deepening the denialist praxis of self-citation and hermetic reference among peers. In any case, the CNPH sought to provide a degree of authenticity, awarding prizes to books such as *O livro branco sobre a conspiração mundial* (*The White Book on World Conspiracy*), an anti-Semitic pamphlet by Sérgio Oliveira.

By the end of the lawsuit, Revisão Editora had become the epicenter and main spreader of international denialist literature in Brazil. With the closure of the publishing house and the death of Siegfried Ellwanger in 2010, this phenomenon grew weaker from the perspective of organized denialism. Subsequently, some exclusively virtual media were developed to reawaken the Revisão Editora legacy, such as websites *Inacreditável* (Unbelievable) and *O Sentinela* (The Sentinel), though both have low international visibility. That does not mean denialism has disappeared from the Brazilian public debate; still, it has lost its characteristic as an organized group, instead opting for widespread dissemination on social networks, for example.

2.4 Neo-Nazism

The third trend of the first phase of neofascism in Brazil was neo-Nazism. Given their ideological and strategic proximity, the relationship between neo-Nazism and some exponents of Holocaust denialism has always been strong; thus, arguably, denialism served as a platform to spread the neo-Nazi doctrine as well as attract individuals to join the neo-Nazi camp.

Despite this relationship, it is necessary to separate the two fields: Holocaust denialism was not restricted *solely* to neo-Nazism but was instead grounded on anti-Semitism to find a shared ground for "classic" anti-Semites and newer exponents of denialism. After all, it was possible to be anti-Semitic and simultaneously pro-Nazism, pro-integralism, or even part of left-wing extremism, among others. On the other hand, neo-integralism tried to approach denialist spaces, mainly based on their relationship with Anésio Lara and the second Brazilian Integralist Action, but this led to no changes in the neo-integralism doctrine of those groups.

Concerning the neo-Nazi field, it is necessary to distinguish two (eventually complementary) areas: the alleged formal initiatives, and the formation of a publicly neo-Nazi skinhead scene, or simply "White Power."

The leading enthusiast of the "institutional" front of Brazilian neo-Nazism was Armando Zanine Júnior, a retired soldier from the Brazilian Merchant Navy, who attempted to found the Brazilian National Socialist Party (Partido Nacional Socialista Brasileiro, PNSB) in 1988, clearly inspired by German national socialism and its racist and anti-Semitic theses. He advocated for agrarian reform, the death penalty as a punishment for corruption crimes, and the principles of eugenics as a tool for improving Brazilian society. Although Zanine stated that he, in theory, opposed racially based differentiation, he publicly preached national–socialist ideals and defended Adolf Hitler. He planned to follow the British example (namely the National Front) by co-opting young skinheads, to no avail. The electoral court denied the PNSB registration request as the legislation prohibited entities that disseminated racist content. Moreover, the movement became void due to the clearly racist discourse and the antiauthoritarian sentiment of the period.

Armando Zanine tried to establish an alternate party for the Brazilian neofascist camp during the democratic transition, but this was not his only political initiative. During the dictatorship, Zanine, like Salgado, was a member of the National Renewal Alliance (Arena), which supported the military regime. In 1966, he was a candidate for state deputy for Rio de Janeiro but was not elected. Still, during the 1960s Zanine founded the Patriotic Phalanx (Falange Patriótica), a fascist-inspired, anticommunist organization that lasted until the 1980s. The degree of irrelevance of neofascism during the 1960s was fundamental to it being ostracized. In 1982, Zanine joined the Social Democratic Party (Partido Democrático Social), the political heir of the Arena party, and once again ran for state deputy.

After the democratic transition, Zanine focused on articulating a field in which he could be the undisputed leader – namely, neo-Nazism. In addition to the attempt to create the PNSB, Armando Zanine established the Brazilian Revolutionary Nationalist Party (Partido Nacionalista Revolucionário Brasileiro, PNRB) in the early 1990s, another party with neo-Nazi leanings. Part of these two initiatives was the usage of newspapers and newsletters as a way of publicizing the cause. One of these was the newspaper *Pátria Livre* (*Free Homeland*), which had the motto "Ou ficar a pátria livre ou morrer pelo Brasil" ("Either the country is free or I die for Brazil," taken from the Brazilian "Independence Anthem") and was distributed in the Brazilian southern and southeastern state capitals. In Curitiba, the newspaper was reported to the Federal Police. Although the complaint filed by the Union of Professional

Journalists of Paraná was motivated by the neo-Nazi content of the newspaper, the argument used to report it was the absence of professional journalists on its staff.

For both the PNSB and the PNRB, Zanine's experience was both brief and illegal, which is a testament to how inviable it was to establish a neo-Nazi party in Brazil. In this respect, the Brazilian experience was different from some cases observed in neighboring countries such as Paraguay (Partido Nacional Socialista Paraguayo, 1989–1993) and Argentina (Partido Nuevo Triunfo, 1990–2009), which had neo-Nazi parties regularly registered in their democratic electoral system.

Regarding skinheads, it is crucial to consider the overarching context. Initially, the approximation between skinheads and neofascism happened based on their shared relationship with the neo-integralist camp. The Carecas were largely influenced by their dialogue with the group led by Anésio Lara Campos, as well as by aspects of integralism that fit with the ethnic diversity of a group like theirs. However, the radicalization process of these skinheads created internal dissent that gradually grew apart from the aesthetic and identity of non-Brazilian neo-Nazi skinheads.

After an internal split in the Carecas, dissidents began incorporating Nazi ideals, identifying with its symbolism, and creating slogans such as "Em defesa da Raça Paulista" ("In defense of the Race from São Paulo") and "Poder Branco" ("White Power"). Initially, they used this symbolism to reinforce the radical leanings of the group and, later, to impose their authority by employing physical, verbal, and symbolic violence, mainly through physical attacks on the streets of large Brazilian cities, constantly challenging other groups, including neo-integralist skinheads (Almeida, 2004).

The incorporation of the swastika and the Celtic cross and the presence of Nazi ideology among the Carecas do Subúrbio stirred internal conflicts, as part of the group was against basing the group's identity primarily on racial segregation. They assumed that racism in Brazil would be unfeasible, given the degree of miscegenation and the myth of racial democracy that the country was intertwined with.

In any case, it is essential to note that prejudiced arguments were fully disseminated in the group's daily life. Although many of the Carecas were not explicitly racist, a number of them were critical of the migrants from the northeast in the south and southeast regions of Brazil. In addition to prejudice against Northeasterners, anti-Semitism and, above all, homophobia were also common. That was the internal dispute that led to the creation of Poder Branco (literally "White Power"), an exclusively neo-nazi skinhead organization.

White Power skinheads gained autonomy from the Carecas by introducing Nazi symbolism in fanzines produced by the group, using the Nazi salute, and vetting the admission of black people in the organization. Thus, the neo-Nazi skinheads grew more autonomous, independent, and intolerant. This strategy had immediate results.

In several states throughout Brazil – notably in the south and southeast regions – White Power skinhead groups began to emerge. White Power skinheads claimed to be the "heirs" of European genetic heritage and superior even to neo-integralist skinheads. Thus, the other majority ethnicities present in Brazil were qualified as pests and leeches, as the neo-Nazis argued that they destroyed and corrupted the communities they lived in.

As dissidents from the neo-integralist skinhead scene, neo-Nazi skinheads needed to impose their autonomy. The strategy they chose was to establish dialogues internationally, in addition to using aggression (and even physical violence) as a demonstration of power between peers. In this way, neo-Nazi skinheads sought to interact with Latin American and European groups. This "Naziskin" scenario led to at least two ventures into the world of international skinhead neo-Nazism. A significant event was the creation of a Brazilian branch of Blood and Honour, a British neo-Nazi group founded by Ian Stuart, linked to the band Skrewdriver (the first Naziskin band to gain visibility on a global scale).

Apparently, the Brazilian branch emerged as a byproduct of the transnational approach of the (minute) Latin America faction, among which Argentina and Chile were more developed (Alcantara, 2015) and even more recognized by the British core group. On the *Blood and Honour* website, they presented themselves as the São Paulo/Argentina division and highlighted the ethnic aspect as a relevant component of this association: "All of them are descendants of Europeans and have been involved in the movement for many years," they stated, just as they sought to establish an idea of racial purity in contrast to other regions of the country: "Brazil is too large a country (with an extension bigger than the whole European continent . . . the population in the northern part of Brazil is mainly non-white. Therefore, it would be illogical to open a B&H; division denominated by their country of origin (Brazil)."

The collaboration between Naziskin groups in Brazil and Argentina was indeed an alternative these small Brazilian groups found to set themselves apart from local difficulties, such as the multiethnic status of the absolute majority of the Brazilian population. For example, the group Divisão 18 (Division 18, a numerical reference to Adolf Hitler's initials) was a brief Naziskin organization that was active in both Argentina and Brazil (Almeida, 2013).

In the early stages of neo-Nazism in Brazil, contact between the two trends of Brazilian neo-Nazism was sparse. Strictly speaking, the main intersection between them was the topic of Holocaust denial. In media events, TV programs, and public debates, they echoed the articulation between Armando Zanine's groups, skinhead leaders, and Siegfried Ellwanger. However, after the Revisão Editora lawsuit and cases of violence and murders associated with skinheads, these groups left the public scene and continued to operate in marginal spaces. White Power skinheads are still active to this day, with a recent attempt in 2023 to create a Brazilian branch of the transnational group Hammerskins involving Brazilian, Argentine, and Portuguese skinheads. Despite this, organized neo-Nazi groups have generally become the most marginal part of the neofascist camp. Armando Zanine stepped away from the political scene, and some neofascist blogs indicate he died in 2018.

The first neofascist wave in Brazil was relevant for testing new trends, crystallizing historically rooted elements, and establishing the outlines of different types of groups. In addition to aspects related to the formation of the neofascist camp, the national political climate also impacted this process. An important aspect that should be noted regarding the first phase of neofascism is the relationship between the democratic transition and the challenges that the various strands faced in articulating themselves.

It is arguable that a low level of internationalization marked the first neofascist wave despite some attempts to establish relations with international groups. In terms of political articulation, neo-integralism was the most prominent trend. That was also due to the presence of integralism in the political culture and the imaginary of the Brazilian extreme right. Concerning internationalization, Holocaust denial was the most prominent topic due to it being a global phenomenon. Even so, this dialogue was hindered by technical, political, and legal difficulties.

As the internet – which was only timidly used by these groups – grew more popular, Brazilian neofascism entered a new phase, marked by the continuity of the three consolidated "traditions" but also incorporating other agendas, such as metapolitics, discussions around identitarian movements, and the arrival of the Fourth Political Theory (by Aleksandr Dugin) in Brazil. Thus, neofascism becomes simultaneously more plural and internationally articulated, leading to the second neofascist wave.

3 The Second Neofascist Wave (2000–2020)

The second phase of neofascism intensified the internationalization process, but there were some setbacks in the integration process amidst the context of international neofascism. In fact, the second phase of neofascism was characterized by a search for international dialogue alongside the upkeeping of historically constructed standards, like in the first phase.

The twenty-first-century neofascist scene in Brazil is strongly inclined toward a global perspective, including for political needs, given that a similar phenomenon can be observed in other far-right spaces. That even motivated some adaptations from neo-integralism, which has traditionally been oblivious or little inclined to establish international dialogues. Even with the persistent hegemony of the Brazilian Integralist Front since the 2000s, new trends and groups have developed an updated repertoire.

The Nationalist Front (Frente Nacionalista), for example, was a neo-integralist group that lasted for a few months between 2014 and 2015. The group was active in the city of Curitiba and claimed a mostly integralist identity, but also had connections with Italian fascism. Concerning neofascism, the group simultaneously nodded to the Italian CasaPound and the Ukrainian Azov Brigade. In fact, the group's symbol was an adaptation of the Azov Brigade's symbol using the Brazilian national colors. The Nationalist Front was one of the first groups of the Brazilian extreme right in the years 2010–2020 to call for the "Ukrainization" of Brazilian politics – which, in the group's view, meant following a revolutionary and antiliberal political proposal with potentially paramilitary purposes.

The new repertoire of neofascism was associated with a broader phenomenon – namely, internationalization initiatives, their results, and the appropriation of new ideas. More than a residual movement, it was marked by the emergence of new groups with new repertoires and identities, some of them openly inspired by the metapolitical matrix of neofascism, which was a common strategy for groups philosophically inspired by Alain de Benoist's French Nouvelle Droite.

This framework can be analyzed based on the actions of the following groups: The neo-integralist Arcy Lopes Estrella Civic-Cultural Association (Associação Cívico Cultural Arcy Lopes Estrella, ACCALE); the national-revolutionary New Resistance (Nova Resistência, NR), which was linked to the Fourth Political Theory; the Identitarian Legion (Legião Identitária) and its associations to extreme right-wing identitarianism; and the Iron Dawn (Aurora de Ferro), inspired by Guillaume Faye's archeofuturism and the French Nouvelle Droite.

ACCALE was officially founded in 2017. The group, whose name is a tribute to the person responsible for the Plínio Salgado Cultural Center in the 1980s, sought to expand interactions in the neofascist field, expanding beyond neo-integralism. Combining integralist ideology with other expressions of the Brazilian radical right (such as Enéas Carneiro's Partido de Reedificação da Ordem Nacional [Party of the Reconstruction of the National Order]), the group adopted a youthful aesthetic mainly inspired by the Italian CasaPound and the tactics of neofascist ultras. In fact, the group makes a pointed nod to an

"Evolian" dimension of neofascism inspired by philosopher Julius Evola. In aesthetic terms, the group let go of the green shirts and instead wore clothing and displayed other visual signs bearing the phrase "Revolt Against the Modern World" – the title of Evola's main book.

The New Resistance is a group inspired by the Nouvelle Resistánce, a French national-revolutionary neofascist group founded by Christian Bouchet in 1991. The group's doctrine focused on the ideas of Russian philosopher Aleksandr Dugin and ideological synthesis strategies (i.e., seeking to incorporate topics from the left and right to consolidate a Fourth Political Theory). Thus, in addition to being national-revolutionary, the group also encompasses neo-Eurasian and national-Bolshevik inspirations. However, this is not a mere import from the French or Russian statute, as it also included adaptations based on the Brazilian ethnic and political reality, such as incorporating topics like miscegenation, religion, and diverse folkloric inspirations. In fact, the New Resistance was a well-articulated expression of Brazilian neofascism, in terms of structure (events, street protests, permeation in a country of continental proportions) as well as in international dialogue.

The Identitarian Legion, founded in 2016, and the Iron Dawn, active since 2018, are two attempts to articulate groups inspired mainly by intellectuals connected to the French Nouvelle Droite. The Nouvelle Droite (and the new European right) are not restricted to the neofascist camp; however, in Brazil, these groups have articulated their ideas. The Identitarian Legion sought to develop activities linked to the global phenomenon of identitarianism (Zúquete, 2018), while the Iron Dawn emerged in connection to the archeofuturism of Guillaume Faye, who, in turn, is also related to the ideology of the Nouvelle Droite.

These new trends impacted the Brazilian neofascist perspective on national identity. As stated earlier, the first phase of neo-integralism was a continuity of historical integralism, based on a procedural and ideological framework that praised the myth of racial democracy – namely, the idea that Brazil is fundamentally void of racism and a place of racial harmony since the colonization (and slavery) process. Thus, issues such as race, ethnicity, and identity were secondary in the neo-integralist universe, although they were recurrent in neo-Nazi discourse.

That had implications for the international ambitions of Brazilian neofascism, which, since the 1960s, has incorporated into its agendas topics such as ethno-differentialism, criticism of multiculturalism, and the right to difference. In short, Brazilian groups were not able to dismiss the issues of identity and metapolitics, leading to new types of neofascist organizations. Therefore, in addition to the period (i.e., late neofascism), there are three other characteristics that justify the isolated nature of Brazilian neofascism.

The first was the marginal role of the nonmilitary extreme right, especially neofascist groups, which had to organize themselves during a democratic transition. The second was that this articulation, which in theory would lead to the establishment of international connections, coincided with a turn toward ethno-differentialism and Eurocentricity by those in Europe, particularly Portugal (Marchi, 2015), who had previously acted as interlocutors for the Latin American groups. In fact, the Portuguese extreme right turned itself inwards to the European continent, reducing the importance of the former Portuguese-speaking spaces in its political imaginary. Finally, the third characteristic was that the internationalization attempts, initially based on neo-Nazism and Holocaust denialism, did not achieve the expected results, whether for intrinsic reasons within the groups or due to the low level of receptivity of potential interlocutors.

3.1 Metapolitics, Identitarianism, and the Fourth Political Theory

Although metapolitics, extreme-right identitarianism, and the Fourth Political Theory are issues that extend beyond neofascism, in Brazil they were imported and appropriated by neofascist groups. The outcomes of this only became evident in Brazilian neofascism in the first decades of the twenty-first century. The situation changed when new technologies became standard and these groups developed a more extensive presence on the internet. This relationship was as follows: at first, neofascist groups began to mention and incorporate authors from the French Nouvelle Droite, especially Alain de Benoist. Based on these connections to this literature, strategic issues (such as right-wing "Gramscism") and ideological issues (like the appeal to identity) became recurrent in the local neofascist camp.

That led to the formation of proper identitarian groups and discussions around identity – and identitarianism – in consolidated groups. At the same time, the new standards enabled Brazilian groups to enter other international neofascist spaces, even outside Europe.

From the 2000s onwards, intellectuals from the Nouvelle Droite started to be mentioned in the Brazilian groupuscular right (Griffin 2003), especially in the neofascist universe. In fact, although the Nouvelle Droite is beyond the neofascist camp, its initial dissemination in Brazil occurred in precisely this scenario. The first mention of Alain de Benoist in Brazil likely happened in 2005, during one of the presentations of the First Integralist Congress of the 21st Century. From the second half of the 2000s onwards, concrete signs of the incorporation of new authors and dynamics began to emerge based on the discussion of Julius Evola's texts and the consolidation of "Evolian" spaces, like the National Evolian Meetings (Encontros Nacionais Evolianos), which were hosted between 2009 and 2014, acting as ways to spread ideology and connect the various groups that attended. In fact, the Evolian events brought together a public interested in traditionalist studies, such as perennialists, dissidents, and, mainly, those related to the Fourth Political Theory of Aleksander Dugin (Valdez, 2024). These were major moments for the Brazilan neofascist right to incorporate elements from neo-Eurasianism and the new French right. The Evolian events were attended by Aleksander Dugin, Alain Soral, and the Argentine dissident philosopher Alberto Buela, thus incorporating a solid element of transnationalism between Latin America and Europe. The notion of multipolarity, the criticism of Atlanticism, an appeal to Third Worldism, as well as the lack of a pan-European sense were factors that helped promote the Fourth Political Theory in Brazil. These are some of the reasons that aid in an understanding of the importance of the Fourth Political Theory in this new phase of neofascism in Brazil.

Effectively, Brazilian neofascism began to be formed under the influence of neo-Eurasian thought, including the creation of a small publishing house (Editora Austral, 2012), whose first book was the translation of a work by Aleksander Dugin (*A Fourth Political Theory* and *Geopolitics of a Multipolar World*) and Julius Evola (*Heathen Imperialism*).

The Brazilian neofascist camp, which had previously been reduced almost exclusively to an homage to its fascist past, started developing new strategies and establishing connections internationally. One of the main results of this newly-updated doctrine and transnational dialogue was the founding of the New Resistance (Nova Resistência, NR). In this context, neo-integralism also took advantage of the transnational enthusiasm that was fomenting, mainly from groups like ACCALE. The last outcome was the creation of other, solely virtual, small organizations, such as the Identitarian Legion (2016) and the Iron Dawn (2018). That marked the end of neofascism as an almost exclusively neo-integralist field.

It was from this moment on that the issues of identity and identitarianism began to circulate more fervently in neofascist spaces, incorporating criticism of the notion of miscegenation as a defining (or limiting) aspect of Brazilian national identity. In addition to the myth of racial democracy and nationalism guided by conservative sociology, the groups and their identity found new grounds to base their dynamics on.

However, there are fractures in this movement. On the one hand, groups such as ACCALE established a relationship with the legacy of integralism. Opposed to the central role that integralism played on the Brazilian identity matrix, other groups, like the Identitarian Legion and the Iron Dawn, incorporated the Nouvelle Droite and the archeofuturism of Guillaume Faye. Finally, the New Resistance became the proponents of the Fourth Political Theory.

3.2 Identities Under Dispute

From the onset of the "identity issue" in the neofascist camp, groups have proposed different readings to justify their autonomy in the debate. For neo-integralists, the leading exponent of this discussion is ACCALE, whose doctrinal guidebook advocates for the search for a national identity and the Brazilian civilizational myth, heavily influenced by historical integralism. This influence is also evident in the way the group seeks to protect Brazilian cultural traditions.

In regards to folklore, the group incorporates the works of Câmara Cascudo, a historical integralist, based on a perspective that considers the existence of different folklore traditions in the country alongside Indigenous contributions and the importance of Christian eschatology. For the group, folklore studies are a political tool against the internationalism of the media and social networks, which supposedly seeks to deter national cultural, political, or economic sovereignty.

Although they nod to a medieval and Christian past in the formation of the Brazilian identity, ACCALE's primary concern is to promote a sense of identity around the amalgamated and native expression of Brazilian nationality. Thus, the group holds the influence of integralist thought and the myth of racial democracy in high regard, which is apparent by their secondary reproduction of texts by authors such as Alain de Benoist, despite still considering Brazilian fascism its central pillar.

Regarding the diverse array of ethnic identities in Brazil, ACCALE advocates for "differentiation in unity," an idea that originated from the 1932 integralism guidelines. The concept is that Brazil, as a country of continental proportions, has numerous identities that must be respected amidst a political centralization process. This perspective is clearly in opposition to separatist movements such as "O Sul é meu País" (The South is my country). As an alternative to separatism and segmented identities, ACCALE seeks totality through an "internal revolution," similar to the integralists. In other words, the Brazilian identity must be derived from "integral humanity" as built by an integralist totalitarian State.

The New Resistance, in turn, incorporates some of the ACCALE's neo-integralist values, such as a critical perspective of separatism. However, this shared view is adopted based on the Fourth Political Theory. While the topic of identity is minor among the goals of the integralist-leaning group, which defines itself as national-revolutionary, it is routinely addressed by its members.

While ACCALE is directed toward a homogenizing notion of identities based on a construct surrounding the formation of an integralist identity to resolve regional differences, the NR praises regional traditions and regionalisms. Regarding the rites of the Gaucho traditions, common to the southern states of Brazil (Rio Grande do Sul, Santa Catarina, and Paraná), NR celebrates these festivities thanks to the knowledge that these communities have regarding the roots and identities of the Gaucho people.

However, there is no mention of separatist ambitions since the Gaucho tradition is seen as part of a whole. The groups state: "Our spirit is Iberian and Guarani, our pride is warrior-like, combative, and pastoral." New Resistance treats any criticism of traditional Gaucho festivities as the byproduct of resentful, materialistic people who follow a globalist agenda that denies native traditions in favor of an artificial, Anglo-Saxon, dominant culture.

The topic of pan-identities, as NR calls it, is of particular concern given the diversity of ethnicities and traditions in the country, and in Latin America more generally. It does not encompass the meaning of amalgamation (like the integralist perspective), nor does it celebrate the efforts of nationalization. This diagnosis is corroborated in texts by Alberto Buela that address Alain de Benoist's assumptions about the plurality of identities and the need to maintain them. Likewise, they are guided by Aleksander Dugin on the issue of having to help identities resist against Western influences, which would supposedly seek to promote an external, artificial, and mechanical identity.

In this sense, the NR does not aim to establish one national identity but rather several aligning identities to fight against the West and a "globalist agenda." Thus, NR criticizes parts of the right that consider the ways of Indigenous peoples to be backward. New Resistance's position on this topic reveals some of the group's ambivalences, which are sometimes closer to parts of the Brazilian extreme right and, at others, are associated with agendas traditionally linked to left-wing social movements. This double-sidedness is one of the defining characteristics of the group and its international interactions; it has been present since its origins, encompassing the French matrix (Bale, 2002), the Fourth Political Theory, and national Bolshevism.

Regarding immigration, the group incorporates some of the arguments of the Brazilian radical right, namely the rejection of free immigration of Venezuelans in the north of the country, despite not considering this a nationwide problem. The search for a sense of multipolarity and appreciation for diverse identities makes the group move away from praise of European traits in the formation of Brazilian identity.

This "amplitude of identities" enables the New Resistance to establish a dialogue with other identitarian groups, as well as a transnational space for neofascism. In 2021, for example, New Resistance held the group's II National Congress, which was praised by a wide variety of leaders and members of international groups, including Latin American ones. Among them, it is possible to highlight names such as Aleksandr Dugin, Christian Bouchet, Luca Boniardi (Radio Fenice Europa), Enrique D'Acedo (Editora Fides), Maxence Smaniotto (Revista Rébellion), Alejandro Vasquez, and Israel Lira (Centro de Estudios Crisolistas and Juventud Nacionalista of Peru), Carlos Salazar (Círculo Patriótico de Estudos Chilenos e Indo-Americanos), José Alsina Calvés (Revista Nihil Obstat), Mickael (Egalité et Réconciliation), and Manuel Rezende (Escudo Identitário), among others.

While ACCALE and NR seek a sense of native identity and the assimilation of a wide array of ethnic nuances, other groups take a more restrictive position in terms of practices and readings surrounding global identitarianism. In short, they are groups that seek to celebrate a European identity in Brazil. The Identitarian Legion is the most prominent example of this.

Created by students from the state of Santa Catarina (Shigunov, 2021) in 2016 and running until 2021, the Identitarian Legion defined itself as a movement aimed at preserving and strengthening the identity and culture of European descendants in the south of Brazil. The group tried to establish a youth-led think tank to influence public opinion in the south of the country. Their symbol was the stylized algiz rune, a nod to the group's connection with the sacred and simultaneously an image that resembles the Araucaria, a tree typical of southern Brazil.

The Identitarian Legion published texts and videos on social media in praise of the white man archetype (the virile warrior), claiming a historical and lasting bond with the European continent. It should be noted that the southern region of Brazil, notably the self-titled European Valley of Santa Catarina, is a region with a solid history of German, Polish, and Italian immigration. Furthermore, the architectural references and some of the region's festivities, such as Oktoberfest (celebrated in cities such as Blumenau, Santa Catarina) gave rise to a sense of a regional identity separate from Brazil on cultural, ethnic, and social grounds. As such, separatism, like that of the "The South is my country," was fervently supported by the Identitarian Legion.

The notion of ancestry as a palingenetic myth (Griffin, 1991) was one of the core elements of the group, which rejected any aspect of miscegenation or Brazilianness and proudly asserted their European origins and roots. The group's manifestos had catchphrases such as "We will not remain silent in the face of the cries of 'you are mestizo, Latino, Brazilian!'" and "We are of

European descent. Nobody has the right to say otherwise. Our culture is a synthesis of different cultures from the European continent."

This "Europeanism" was evident in the group's texts and ideological patterns. While others, like the New Resistance, incorporated the principles of the Fourth Political Theory, the Identitarian Legion spread texts not only by Julius Evola but also by Dominique Venner, Alain de Benoist, and Guillaume Faye. Other noncentral topics for other identitarian groups, such as concerns about mass immigration and the dangers of "Islamization," were spread by the Identitarian Legion as a way of establishing a symbiotic relationship between the south of Brazil and Europe, emulating a supposedly intercontinental and transatlantic argumentation.

However, the movement's attempt to establish a connection between European identitarianism and white identitarianism in southern Brazil had no success. The initiative, which included an imprint (Aquiles) and the translation of books by Mark Willinger (*Generation Identity: A Declaration of War Against the '68ers*) and Alain de Benoist and Charles Champetier (*Manifesto for a European Renaissance*), was restricted to the internet and, as such, ephemeral. The group even argued against accusations that it was an exclusively online movement. That was done by resorting to Jack Donovan's views about the internet as a cultural war tool; however, the group did cease its operations, which happened exclusively online.

Another active group, the Iron Dawn, which originated after internal turmoil in the New Resistance, also leveraged European identitarianism. Similarly operating exclusively online, the group is inspired by its North American counterpart, the "Archeofuturist Front," which is itself inspired by the ideas of the French Nouvelle Droite and, mainly, by the archeofuturism of Guillaume Faye. The Iron Dawn partnered with ACCALE and simultaneously incorporated European and Indigenous elements to develop an identity archetype for Brazilian civilization.

The group claims to adopt a diffuse and multiethnic sense of identity, being descended from warriors and conquerors, based on an assortment of various origins, such as *bandeirantes* (figures associated with the colonial enterprise), Tupi-Guarani Indigenous warriors, and enslaved Yoruba people. Despite the references to Indigenous and enslaved black people, the group is centered around the cult of the white colonizers and the *bandeirante* conquerors, represented as a synthesis of the warrior, the explorer, and the dominator – that is, the true national identity.

The group's founding document, "Manifesto for a New Rome," stated that Brazil had a connection with the knights of the Order of Christ and the Templars, making up "the Portuguese heritage of the Fifth Empire ... there is something metaphysical and ancient in this soil and in the blood of the people who live here." The celebration of the *bandeirantes* is based on miscegenation, but with the Portuguese over other people.

The group is similar to ACCALE or even the New Resistance in their search for a native and ethnically mixed dimension of identitarianism but attributes a central role to European identities. And although it doesn't make use of/defend the notion of pan-identitarianism like the New Resistance, neither does it defend a Europeanist perspective, like the Identitarian Legion.

It can be said that the theme of identity and groups based on identitarianism caused divergences throughout the second wave of Brazilian neofascism. Although it is still disputed issue, it highlights how the neofascist camp has become more varied and internationalized in recent decades. This process is limited in some spheres, such as the discussion about the Islamization of Europe, which is not a concrete reality in the Brazilian political scene because the "danger" of Islamization is not a common theme among the Brazilian extreme right, in addition to the obvious fact that Brazil is not a European country.

Despite these distances, and despite its limitations, Brazilian neofascism became a space for intellectual reflection. That enabled it to work with new issues (such as identities) and new geopolitical spaces. This led neofascists and the neofascist scene to develop a level of maturity in relation to the international field, which can be measured by intellectual circulation, as well as by the support (albeit occasional) from international leaders, neofascist organizations and the extreme right.

In contrast, the first phase of neofascism was monopolized by an attempt to maintain neo-integralism, with some marginal neo-Nazi initiatives. Throughout the twenty-first century, Brazilian neofascism has become more plural and diverse. However, this does not mean it is in sync with the European organizations, given that these debates have been occurring since the 1960s and have only recently been incorporated into the Brazilian landscape.

Beyond the intellectual and ideological perspectives, neofascism also became a recurring political player, surpassing the marginal status of being a seemingly anachronistic organization. This political impact resulted from these groups' intellectual maturation, international dialogue, and development, but the broader political framework also played a part. Therefore, it is important to understand where, how, and when neofascism will establish a dialogue with the Brazilian far right.

4 Dialogues between Neofascism and the Brazilian Far Right

It is essential to consider that neofascism is a particular phenomenon within a broader field: the Brazilian far right. This understanding enables us to presume the existence of a radical right, whose demands, proposals, and political values converge with those of the extreme right, despite their disagreements regarding their procedural stance on liberal democracy (Mudde, 2019). The extreme right, which rejects and actively opposes democracy (to the point of publicly proposing its extinction), differs from the radical right, which has adapted to the institutional demands and perspectives of democracy, thus effectively competing inside the political game.

It is important to emphasize that institutional structure is not an absolutely definitive aspect of the nature of a given political group. Since the crisis of authoritarian and fascist regimes, many prominent parts of the extreme right have had to adapt to the postfascist political climate without there being any profound change in their ideological standards. In addition to the period when these neofascist groups organized themselves into political parties (mainly in Western Europe), it is prudent to consider the advance of radical right-wing populist parties an interregnum (Traverso, 2018), in the sense that the authoritarian and/or fascist political culture has adapted into a populist formation (Finchelstein, 2019) without publicly claiming the label of "neofascism." In other words, it is possible to state that there are extreme right groups that organize themselves as political parties, just as there are some strands of the radical right that opt for the same strategy.

But how does Brazil fit in this context? Again, it is necessary to consider the political and institutional climate that followed the democratic transition. As the right grew sparse in the national public scene, formal politics became the stage for the "embarrassed right" phenomenon. That meant that right-wing political players were not open about their political stance even after a conservative transition (Power, 2000).

As discussed previously, this lack of political representation was seen as an opportunity for small neofascist groups to articulate themselves while demanding or celebrating authoritarian and antidemocratic advances. However, this also had an impact from an electoral point of view. The "embarrassed right" was the result of an absence of a political project for the Brazilian radical right – and the neofascist camp took notice of that.

As previously stated, both neo-integralists and neo-Nazis tried to articulate neofascist parties. The National Action Party (Partido de Ação Nacional) and the Integralist Action Party (Partido de Ação Integralista) were the leading proponents of neo-integralism. The Brazilian National Socialist Party and the

Brazilian National Revolutionary Party were the two attempts led by Armando Zanine, which were immediately shut down.

In fact, in the 1980s, during the early days of neofascism, there was no concrete possibility for this type of group to have a viable chance in elections, or even any legal recognition, given the antiauthoritarian mechanisms and resources in the new Brazilian constitution. In a country of continental proportions, with only some disjointed activism and a few embryonic initiatives trying to push neofascism forward, its political–electoral impact was effectively negligible.

The decade between the return of multipartyism (1979) and the first direct presidential election (1989) in Brazil was marked by a void of institutional representation from the far right, and not just from neo-fascists. This did not mean there were no politically organized, conservative-leaning agents in political parties, as was the case of deputy Bolsonaro, who moved between several parties at the time. However, the party framework was indeed disjointed. That changed in 1989 with the creation of the Party of the Reconstruction of the National Order (Partido de Reedificação da Ordem Nacional, PRONA).

4.1 PRONA and Neofascism

The PRONA party was led by Enéas Ferreira Carneiro, a cardiologist with military training born in the north of the country, with no political career until the moment he founded the party and ran as a presidential candidate (which happened in the same year).

At a time when the primary political propaganda tool was free insertion on radio and TV stations, Carneiro became a popular figure. Each party's parliamentary share defined the time available for each candidate, thus new parties had very brief appearances. Although he only had 15 seconds in the Free Electoral Broadcast Airtime, Carneiro attracted attention. He was somewhat of a caricature, with his bald head, long beard, and thick-rimmed glasses. In political propaganda pieces, he appeared in slightly improvised scenarios, with a tone of voice that expressed authority, incisiveness and accelerated speed. His discourse outlined a path toward a nationalist, authoritarian, conservative, and moralist project. In short, he delivered a proposal that the Brazilian far right, including neofascist organizations, could get behind.

In the 1989 electoral campaign, Carneiro criticized the Constituent Assembly, career politics, and his opponents' campaigns. He denounced an orchestrated farce against the Brazilian people and called for votes in terms such as "If you believed me, protest against everything that is out there. Vote to put an end to disorder! Take a deep breath, puff your chest, and shout out alongside the entirety of Brazil: My name is Enéas!"

His slogan "My name is Enéas" (in Portuguese, "Meu nome é Enéas"), combined with political discontent, was a prominent feature in a presidential election campaign that, in 1989, had more than twenty candidates. Furthermore, the fact that Carneiro (and PRONA) claimed to have no ties to career politics enabled him to put forward a narrative in which he presented himself as an outsider. These factors shot Carneiro to fame, although his appearance and his electoral strategy were usually subject to humorous and mocking remarks.

Beyond the aesthetic issue there was his political nature, which filled a void that had perpetuated since the consolidation of the "embarrassed right." The authoritarian discourse, his eulogy for order, and the denunciation of a moral and customs crisis helped him establish a place in the conservative camp, while also pleasing several parts of the Brazilian extreme right (Caldeira Neto, 2017).

However, PRONA grew as a radical right party and had the potential to become a reference for the Brazilian extreme right. Even so, this growth should not be understood simply as a mechanical relationship between the discourse of its leadership and the wishes of certain sectors of the political field. Firstly, it is necessary to understand the vacancy in the Brazilian right that PRONA actively sought to occupy. This process began after the founding of the party, Carneiro's first candidacy in 1989, and the path to the subsequent electoral process in 1994.

After 1989, while PRONA was becoming stronger politically, there are two other contextual elements that should be considered. The first was the political crisis triggered by the impeachment of President Fernando Collor de Mello for his involvement in corruption scandals. Amidst this, Carneiro's portrayal as an outsider served as a critique of career politics and a reactive alternative to the discontent from the fall of the first directly elected president since the end of the military regime. Furthermore, Carneiro's nationalist discourse outlined the potential for new economic policies opposed to the Washington Consensus and its neo-liberal measures, especially in the context of the Real Plan (Plano Real).

In the political arrangements of nationalist and authoritarian right, PRONA was responsible for articulating the various existing trends, refining their discourse and appeal to order and authority, and unveiling an alleged international conspiracy aimed at destroying Brazil's national sovereignty, the armed forces, and conservative values. To this end, PRONA began advocating for a "strong, technical and intervening" State. This motto was not only a letter of introduction from the party to various sectors of the Brazilian extreme right and authoritarian nationalism, it was also a product, an effective result of this interaction between PRONA and the trends that were considered "dormant" and "alien" in relation to formal politics at the beginning of the New Republic.

In preparation for the 1994 presidential elections, PRONA intensified its relationship with some authoritarian-nationalist political groups, especially those with members of the military who collaborated with the newspaper *Ombro a Ombro*, where several collaborators of the 1994 government program came from, encompassing areas such as the economy, military strategy studies, geopolitics, and mining, as was the case of Rear Admiral Roberto Gama e Silva, Carneiro'scandidate for vice-president.

In addition to the military extreme right, neofascist groups also openly condoned Carneiro's candidacy. Carecas do Subúrbio, for example, stated that the discourse based on patriotism and the cult of authority was aligned with their fundamental political values. And although the ethnic issue was not present in Carneiro's political project, even neo-Nazi groups became interested in establishing ties with PRONA from 1994 onwards. Armando Zanine, for example, claimed that Carneiro's was the only genuinely nationalist candidate, and so he would encourage his alleged followers to vote for him.

When asked by the press, Carneiro's political advisors denied any possibility of approaching the most radical neofascist trends, especially neo-Nazi groups. Although PRONA did not acknowledge support from neo-Nazi groups, it illustrates how representative the party had become, and also how neofascist groups were starting to move toward formal politics. In other words, because they were not able to rally around a fundamentally neofascist political party, they began to connect with established groups to gain representation and also to find similar political projects that converged with the broader field of the Brazilian far right.

Carneiro's efforts, combined with the protest vote for a caricatural and antisystem candidate, proved a political success. Unlike in 1989, when he came twelfth in the election, with 0.5 percent or approximately 360,000 votes, in 1994 Carneiro came third, with more than 4.5 million votes (7.38 percent of the total valid votes). The Brazilian press began to report on what they called the "Enéas danger," and it was not uncommon for Carneiro's to be characterized as a neofascist candidate.

Regardless of how the political ideology of Carneiro and PRONA is characterized – which was closer to authoritarian and conservative nationalism than neofascism or integralism – their relationship with extreme-right organizations empowered future candidacies. In 1998 (the last year in which Carneiro ran for the presidency), his relationship with small extreme right groups intensified. PRONA organized itself to be recognized as the main organization (political party) representing the Brazilian radical right of the period. In addition to parts of the military, Carneiro created connections with conservative antiabortion entities and international organizations such as the Ibero-American Solidarity Movement – the main branch of Lyndon LaRouche's organization in Brazil. That helped intensify the conspiracy-ridden content in Carneiro's discourse. For example, the attacks on George Soros became part of the party's daily political life.

Although PRONA has consolidated itself as the primary reference for the extreme right, it only established relationships with integralist groups from the 2000s onwards. From the neo-integralist perspective, this was the result of internal turmoil due to the "institutional hiatus" of neo-integralism, which, in turn, arose from the power struggles and divergent ideological stances regarding topics such as anti-Semitism and Holocaust denial. Furthermore, there were opposing views regarding strategic issues for twenty-first-century integralism, with many members wanting to effectively step away from formal politics.

As the main neo-integralist organization, the Brazilian Integralist Front invested in a strategic and effective approach with PRONA. The neo-integralist press indicated their votes for Carneiro and other prominent party leaders, seeking to make their relationship with the group public. Contrary to the attempt to approach neo-Nazi entities, when the neo-integralists tried to establish a connection Carneiro welcomed them. Publicly, Carneiro stated that there were similarities between PRONA, a nationalist party, and historical integralism.

In 2002, Carneiro decided to run for Federal Deputy and received an astonishing 1.57 million votes, setting a new record at the time. Carneiro's votes helped elect Elimar Damasceno, who had ties to the Brazilian Integralist Front, as Federal Deputy. This marked the return of integralism to the Chamber of Deputies.

In his mandate, Damasceno advocated for the integralist memory and addressed groups and demands from the military extreme right while also promoting an antirights agenda on issues such as reproductive rights and access to abortion. Damasceno's mandate also enabled party deputies and other extreme-right leaders, such as Bolsonaro, to rally around demands related to the memory of the battles that occurred during the military regime. Damasceno's main advisor was Paulo Fernando da Costa, a lawyer who, at the time, was one of the main leaders of the Brazilian Integralist Front and a growing figure in the neo-integralist scene.

This convergence between PRONA and neo-integralism was the party's final episode. PRONA was extinguished in 2006, thus frustrating all neofascist plans and ambitions. It then merged with the Liberal Party (Partido Liberal), leading to the creation of the Republic Party (Partido da República). Carneiro initiated this process. At the time, he was struggling both with his health and with political issues that arose from a new electoral legislation, which was not very beneficial to small parties. He was re-elected as a deputy in 2006, but did not complete his mandate as he died in 2007. The death of Carneiro was traumatic for the Brazilian far right, which started calling him "the best president Brazil never had." Associating oneself with the memory of Carneiro essentially became a sign of one's defense of the far right and authoritarian nationalism, on top of being, not infrequently, an effective nod to neofascist groups.

4.2 The New Right-Wing, Neofascism, and Bolsonarism

The end of PRONA created an empty space in Brazilian far-right representation, but the context became more diverse. From 2011 onwards, the right-wing grew politically more robust in the public space. In practical terms, the "embarrassed right" had come to a definite end, and the Brazilian political and social fields were open to new groups and trends that felt proud to declare themselves right wing.

For these groups, being on the right meant being part of a wider group. They often agree on conservative values, which usually involve religious expression (Catholic or Evangelical), opposition to the left (and particularly the PT), repudiation of quota policies, and the clash against social movements (particularly feminism), defense of guns, agribusiness, and so forth.

The new rights are not restricted to only one ideological bloc or political party. Some, for example, operate based on a notion of neo-liberal radicalization (including aspects such as so-called anarcho-capitalism), while others seek more traditionalist models. In summary, the new right wing brought new elements to the conservative agenda, such as the appeal to armamentism, as well as new actors, such as religious groups, notably the evangelicals. However, this plurality of new right-wing movements was also part of a broader history. Regarding conservatism, the moralistic perspective of overseeing women's bodies and advocating for traditional and heteronormative family models was added to the long-established stance against communism. The defense of the free market, even against a supposed authoritarianism, echoed the old political formations, which resonated in the markedly radical contexts and discourses of the Cold War period.

Still, the new political formations and their characteristics cannot be ignored. In addition to using new communication and information technologies, the new Brazilian right-wing movements expanded their bases. They developed a culture of protest around the anticorruption agenda during the crises involving the PT and the growing antipolitical discourse that emerged from Operation Car Wash (Operação Lava Jato) and the judicialization of Brazilian politics. These aspects gradually challenged the foundations of the so-called New Republic, inaugrated after the democratic transition and the National Constituent Assembly. The exhaustion of the commodity cycle and the weakening of the "pink tide" (the wave left-wing governments in Latin America) were also relevant.

The popularization of these new right-wing movements is also connected to the crisis that befell the presidential mandate of Rousseff (Workers' Party), the first woman to be elected president of Brazil. Throughout the Rousseff government, the opposition to policies on human rights (mainly the National Human Rights Program/Programa Nacional de Direitos Humanos, PNDH-3), the memory of the most recent civil–military dictatorship (particularly the National Truth Commission, Comissão Nacional da Verdade), and the fight against homophobia (the Schools Without Homophobia project, Escola Sem Homofobia), consolidated a camp of antirights right-wing movements, as well as a framework with an increasingly violent and antidemocratic appeal within which the far right could thrive.

The activities of the National Truth Commission, for example, intensified the reaction of right-wing military sectors, especially the more radical ones such as Terrorism, Never Again (Terrorismo Nunca Mais), a group that contested the Commission reports and advocated for political ruptures.

In this context of radicalization, some groups tried to create far-right political parties. One example was the idealized "refoundation" of the National Renewal Alliance, in honor of the party that supported the dictatorship that began in 1964, as well as the formation of the Brazilian Military Party (Partido Militar Brasileiro), which presented itself as "the solution to make things right-wing in the country."

Amidst this, Bolsonaro gradually built his presence as a leader. Throughout the 2010s, Bolsonaro occupied the media and the political sphere by leveraging some aspects of the public debate, responding to sparse demands and nods from the military and getting closer to Catholic conservatism, most of all the evangelicals. Bolsonaro's presence at the passing out of military classes, as well as his evangelical baptism at the Jordan River in Israel, illustrate how he moved away from the marginal stronghold of the low-ranking military extreme right and incorporated new rallying and representative elements, mainly based on issues concerning heteronormative sexuality, criticism of quota policies, and religious appeal. Accordingly, he brought back the motto "God, Homeland, Family," once used by Brazilian fascists in the 1930s, which would gain nationwide visibility in the 2018 election.

Bolsonaro got closer to the neofascist camp when he became popular in the far right, occupying a role that had been vacant since the death of Carneiro and the dissolution of PRONA. One of the founding events of Bolsonarism was, possibly, an event from 2011 in which neofascist groups organized a demonstration in São Paulo in favor of the extreme-right deputy. At the time, Bolsonaro was facing accusations of racism and homophobia – topics that were perceived as a concrete way of rallying small neofascist groups, such as the neo-integralist Ultra Defense (Ultra Defesa). Neo-Nazi skinhead groups were also present, such as Kombat RAC (Rock Against Communism).

However, the fact that Bolsonaro became a central figure in Brazilian politics should not be credited to neo-fascists. In fact, Bolsonaro built a career connected to right-wing military extremism. He subsequently got closer to various extreme-right movements (including neo-fascists) and new exponents of the right-wing, such as the Free Brazil Movement (Movimento Brasil Livre, MBL). There is no doubt that several neofascist groups saw Bolsonaro as a first-rate ally. In addition to nationalism, conservatism, and militarism, Bolsonaro built a political career around the denial of the civil–military dictatorship, not infrequently praising torturers. Before establishing a closer relationship with intellectual and traditionalist guru Olavo de Carvalho, Bolsonaro's leading political guru was Carlos Alberto Brilhante Ustra, colonel of the Brazilian Army and head of torture centers during the dictatorship. For neofascist trends, anticommunist political violence was a nod to ideological affinities and enabled them to gain political influence.

However, Bolsonaro had an erratic political history, having moved between almost a dozen political parties. Neofascist groups started supporting Bolsonaro as a potential presidential candidate and began to pave their way into political parties that were adhering to the radical right.

During the political crisis that culminated in the impeachment of Rousseff, smaller parties, such as the Brazilian Labor Renewal Party (Partido Renovador Trabalhista Brasileiro, PRTB) – and its main leader, Levy Fidelix – were moving toward the radical right. To this end, PRTB and Fidelix fostered relationships with extreme-right groups, including neofascist ones such as the Nationalist Front. In addition to the Nationalist Front, which drew inspiration from integralism, the Italian CasaPound, and the Azov Brigade, PRTB also started establishing relationships with the neo-integralist-leaning Carecas. However, the political and media impact of these connections ended up weakening this initial movement.

When Bolsonaro (now affiliated with the tiny Social Liberal Party, Partido Social Liberal) emerged victorious in the presidential election, he also brought PRTB over to the winning side since Hamilton Mourão, a retired general and Bolsonaro's vice-president, was affiliated with PRTB. Throughout the 2018 electoral campaign, the PRTB from São Paulo effectively engaged with the Brazilian Integralist Front. Victor Barbuy, president of Frente Integralista Brasileira (FIB), met publicly with Rodrigo Tavares, the PRTB's governor candidate for São Paulo, and with Fidelix, the party president. On both occasions, the FIB and PRTB leaders were carrying books by the AIB's paramount leader, Plínio Salgado.

Undoubtedly, Bolsonaro was a representative of the more radical parts of the Brazilian extreme right. He had been a politically active figure since the democratic transition and gained prominence for defending torture and other activities incompatible with what is legally acceptable under a democracy, thus fostering disbelief in liberal democracy and institutional rites, on top of spreading contempt for minorities and politically persecuting his opponents. Therefore, it is not surprising that the then deputy Bolsonaro was recognized as a potential leader by many radical groups from the Brazilian extreme right, even neo-fascists.

However, amidst anticommunist rhetoric and radical and intolerant premises, Bolsonaro and his allies were, until very recently, members of the so-called "lower clergy": that is, parliamentarians without much visibility or political power. That was the case even in terms of representation and their relationship with neofascist organizations, which, as mentioned, favored Carneiro's PRONA because it was a more structured political party.

The dizzying rise of Bolsonaro's presidential candidacy in 2018 happened alongside the absence of a robust partisan engine, which would have hindered the integration of neofascist organizations. Initially, Bolsonaro signaled his affiliation with the National Ecological Party (Partido Ecológico Nacional), which, in theory, would change its name to PRONA in honor of Carneiro. Finally, Bolsonaro joined the Free Social Party (Partido Social Livre), a group that did not have a fully defined ideological agenda.

I argue that, on top of how neofascist groups articulated themselves throughout the so-called New Republic, the actions of these new right-wing movements help us provide a more adequate interpretation of how "Bolsonarism" came to be. In other words, neofascist organizations got closer to Bolsonaro – and Bolsonarism – when it was on the rise and amidst the commotion of the new rights, but he is not the direct result of these articulations by neofascist groups given that they have no meaningful political strength.

Furthermore, it is necessary to consider that, throughout the election, Bolsonaro's campaign discourse signaled the emptying of the State, not only socially but also from the perspective of the privatization of state-owned companies in strategic sectors, which in right-wing nationalist rhetoric and imagery would be opposed to the model that neofascist groups sought.

Despite Bolsonaro's prejudiced and intolerant views, some elements of his political project represent the diversity of the new right-wing movements in Brazil. Conspiracy theories (such as "globalism" or "cultural Marxism"), absorbed directly from an imaginary that permeated different sectors of right-wing thought (and also from historical fascism itself), coexist with ultra-liberal economic project and discourse, as well as support for Israel and the USA, especially for the political projects of Benjamin Netanyahu and Donald Trump.

From this perspective, although Bolsonaro's discourse and practices do justice to some key ideas of the Brazilian neofascist-leaning extreme right, at other times they hold opposing views, or at least substantial differences, as is the case with the defense of privatizations.

Not only as a result of disputes between representatives of a specific field but also due to philosophical and ideological issues, such interactions or support from neofascist groups when Bolsonaro was building his electoral campaign must be investigated in light of the interests of these neofascist groups, as well as their similarities and differences. However, pointing out their differences does not mean erasing the similarities between Bolsonaro's supporters, historical fascism, and neofascist groups.

The fact that Bolsonaro publicly used the motto "God, Homeland, Family," which was popular among the integralists, was a sign of their ideological affinity and also acted as a dog whistle for the neofascist camp, which helped radicalize the election in which Bolsonaro emerged victorious.

Likewise, neofascist groups were seeking to get closer to Bolsonaro but also stepped back at strategic moments. After all, being incorporated into Bolsonaro's project could mean giving up their autonomy in favor of groups that had forged their political identities over the last few decades, even establishing ties abroad, however timidly and belatedly.

Still, Bolsonaro's electoral success, the Bolsonaro government, and the phenomenon of Bolsonarism held concrete potential for neofascist groups, and they took this opportunity to articulate and intensify their proposals. These groups have become more radical during Bolsonaro's government.

Neo-integralism, for example, outlined two paths. The first was formal articulation. Paulo Fernando da Costa, who had connections with the Brazilian Integralist Front and had been an advisor under Damasceno (PRONA) in the 2000s, joined the Ministry of Women, Family, and Human Rights as a special advisor under minister and evangelical pastor Damares Alves. Within this ministry, which was previously named the Ministry of Human Rights, Paulo Fernando da Costa was involved in transforming it to prioritize the conservative family model, considered as a "minority" at risk of being extinguished due to the advances of progressive agendas, social movements, feminist groups and entities, LGBTQIA+ organizations, and so forth.

During the 2022 elections, Paulo Fernando da Costa ran for – and was elected as surrogate for – district deputy, with the support of Damares Alves. Asked about her support for an integralist, the minister (and, at the time, an elected senator) praised integralism as a movement defending the ideals of "God, Homeland, Family."

The other path available to neo-integralism was radicalization. In December 2019, a neo-integralist group with a long name (the Nationalist Popular Insurgence Command of the Integralist Brazilian Family, Comando de Insurgência Popular Nacionalista da Família Integralista Brasileira) claimed responsibility for an attack on a comedy production company after the release of a video mocking Christmas. The main person responsible for the attack was Eduardo Fauzi, a neo-integralist activist who had been part of groups such as the Brazilian Integralist Front and ACCALE, among others.

On the other hand, neo-Nazism received some nods from the Bolsonaro government. In January 2020, Culture Secretary Roberto Alvim emulated a textual and visual replica of a speech by Joseph Goebbels, of the Ministry of Propaganda for Nazi Germany. That happened during the release of the Bolsonaro government's cultural plan, which argued that "Brazilian art in the next decade will be heroic and national . . . or else it will be nothing." Alvim's speech should be understood as a dog whistle to the extremists among the broad spectrum of convergence between Bolsonaro and the extreme right – that is, a tool to foster radicalization and loyalty.

Although Alvim was fired, the neo-Nazi scene grew, becoming more widespread during the Bolsonaro government. In contrast to how it initially worked when neo-Nazism was articulated in three structuring themes (skinheads, organized groups, and Holocaust denial) and their respective leadership groups, the most recent phenomenon was more diffuse as it rallied online, using instant messaging apps or even individual actions, including potential lone-wolf terrorism.

In 2021, for example, organizations such as Safernet received 15,000 reports of neo-Nazi activities on the Brazilian internet. This figure represented a 60 percent increase on the number of complaints registered in the previous year. In 2020, the Federal Police increased the number of investigations associated with the spread of neo-Nazism in the country by 59 percent. Between 2010 and 2018, the times series points to thirteen investigations per year, while thirty-six investigations were recorded in the first half of 2021 alone.

However, in addition to the agitation arising from outside formal political spaces, the military also began to adopt some political and aesthetic strategies that were once part of neofascism. Bolsonarism, in effect, demonstrated the capacity to be a broader phenomenon, aggregating various trends, even those closer to neofascism. In his government, Bolsonaro did not necessarily follow what his electorate demanded online and in the streets, namely greater commitment and urgency in proposing more radical measures, especially those that had the potential to cause democratic ruptures.

In recent years, even more radical groups have articulated a varied repertoire inside the spectrum of Bolsonarism. One of these developments was so-called Ukrainization. Ukrainizing groups claimed that this name was inspired by the Euromaidan in Ukraine, when student protests gave way to extreme-right groups. From the perspective of these Brazilian groups, Ukrainization would mean adopting violent tactics to cause tension and purge the political field of their opponents and career politicians. To this end, they organized camps and street demonstrations, with a repertoire of strategies that grew in the following months. As previously stated, strictly speaking the idea of Ukrainization was predominantly linked to small neofascist groups, but it became commonplace in the more radical groups of Bolsonarism, thus promoting an effective dialogue between – or even hybridization of – radical Bolsonarism and neofascism.

There were some actions from neofascist-inspired groups that used the shared aesthetic of extreme-right identitarian groups, as well as those of the American alt-right. One example of this is the Trezentos (Three Hundred), a small group that targeted the Federal Supreme Court and its ministers. This group promoted events using the shared aesthetics of organizations such as the French Génération Identitaire, the Italian CasaPound, and the Unite the Right event held in Charlottesville in 2017.

This type of articulation involved not only incorporating methods used by neofascist groups in other countries but also reproducing an American alt-right aesthetic. In the USA, Trumpist or alt-right aesthetics managed to impact the dynamics of social media and language-related spaces used by other international movements. Memes, some conspiracy theories, and other small-group dynamics acted as a kind of mirror between Bolsonarism, Trumpism, and other extreme-right movements precisely for their attacks on political and electoral formality.

Finally, this also affected the ideologically motivated political violence of everyday life. As stated previously, the use of bombs and politically charged attacks is not new in the daily life of the Brazilian extreme right. The integralists tried to murder Getúlio Vargas in 1938. The military and anticommunist groups came together in the 1970s and 1980s to block the democratic transition process. In 2023, several Bolsonarist and military groups organized a coup attempt in response to the presidential election and inauguration of Luís Inácio Lula da Silva.

However, the current situation encompasses new characteristics that converge with the ideological nature of neofascism, as well as with the shared dynamics of international neofascism in countries such as the USA. In recent years, there has been a consolidation of online spaces worshipping murderers, white supremacists, and mass shooters; this is related to other digital culture niches focused on the use of specific drugs, violent practices, suicide, mutilation, and other elements that lead to a wide range of not only mental health issues but also political ones. The intersection between these two areas is a testament to how neofascism (and, mainly, neo-Nazism) is capable of rallying individuals and being part of their ideological formation. Therefore, this is a new context for the neo-Nazism issue, which is related to the attacks on schools in Brazil.

4.3 A Third Wave?

By definition, these attacks follow the logic of copycat crimes (i.e., in terms of the recurring aspects of the political identities claimed by the attackers and their techniques). Between 2022 and October 2023, there were thirty-six attacks on schools. This situation, which effectively began in 2017, resulted in thirty-eight deaths from firearms and eleven deaths from cold weapons. A 2023 report by the Brazilian federal government and the Work Group of Specialists on Violence in Schools (Grupo de Trabalho de Especialistas em Violências nas Escolas) pointed toward political extremism – particularly neo-Nazism – as a core factor to define the scope of the problem.

That means that, amidst the recent spread of political violence in Brazil, neo-Nazism has consolidated a field for politically, racially, and religiously motivated violence, even employing neofascist terrorism techniques such as "lone wolves." It is also plausible that this is a byproduct of the broader national backdrop of far-right discourse intensification.

Therefore, it is necessary to understand how widespread neo-Nazism has become in Brazil in recent times without focusing solely on government positions. To do this, it is necessary to develop a dialectical analysis framework that investigates how the use of extreme right-wing discourse in formal politics has validated the practices of extreme right-wing groups in nonformal political spaces.

Finally, the most recent movements in neofascism within the Brazilian political field went beyond the limits of the radical and extreme right. New Resistance, a national-revolutionary exponent of the Fourth Political Theory, has employed the tactics of rapprochement and entryism that have been present in European neofascism since the 1970s. As New Resistance leverages a sense of nationalism and anti-imperialism to create a notion of third-worldism close to left-wing trends, it also praises historical figures of the Brazilian far right (Salgado, Carneiro, etc.). This strategy is not exclusive to this Brazilian group and is also part of the identity of the French group with the same name. In recent years, the New Resistance has tried to engage with two parties on the Brazilian left. Their relationship with the Democratic Labor Party (Partido Democrático Trabalhista), the self-proclaimed political heir of left-wing labor movements, was based precisely on developmental, nationalist values that oppose the so-called "identitarian" agendas (LGBTQIA+, feminism, Black movements, etc.). Concerning the far-left Labor's Cause Party (Partido da Causa Operária), their affinities are based on topics such as anti-Zionism, anti-imperialism, and the praise of political violence. This topic is still in development and is criticized by antifascist activists who rally around the "El Coyote" portal and other left-leaning groups.

In general, recent decades have benefited the Brazilian neofascist scene. The expansion of Brazilian neofascism from the second wave onwards and its interaction with the international scene has enabled it to effectively establish a dialogue with the far right. At the same time, the formation of an updated Brazilian radical right with international ties also helped enable this dialogue, especially considering that neofascist groups are helpful for the authoritarian escalation of the Brazilian radical right and other extreme-right movements. After decades of development, Brazilian neofascism found its footing in formal and nonformal spaces.

This naturalization of extreme-right discourse in the Brazilian political and formal space must be understood as a process of legitimization of openly intolerant groups that condone most violent aspects of the extreme right and neo-Nazism, including terrorist tactics. This is built in a space of transnational articulation and on digital platforms, which have set a new standard for racially and ethnically motivated violent extremism in Brazil.

In addition to patterns and strategies that have been consolidated throughout the two major waves of neofascism, new agendas were introduced and mediated via digital platforms and direct messaging apps, such as Telegram, Discord, and X/Twitter, among others. For example, Terrorgram, a recent phenomenon in Brazil, was built globally as a community that spreads hate speech and is often associated with neo-Nazi symbols and values, whilst also encompassing other elements from the global field of right-wing extremism and neofascism.

In general, the Brazilian field seeks to incorporate these agendas and, when possible, adapt these international standards to the Brazilian reality. For example, Southern separatism has been used to propose new fronts for parts of the extreme right that are closer to neofascism, particularly neo-Nazism. Groups such as Falange de Aço (Steel Falange) seek to build an identity that is simultaneously neo-Nazi and separatist, promoting hate speech against Brazilian sexual, ethnic, and regional minorities. In virtual spaces, these initiatives, which have become increasingly common in the recent history of the

Brazilian extreme right, were revamped with new ideological views, such as identitarianism, accelerationism, neoreactionaryism (inspired by authors such as Nick Land and Curtis Yarvin), and archeofuturism, among others.

Even around more traditional trends, such as neo-integralism, the signs of an intensification toward more violent acts have become more noticeable. In recent years, on social media, integralist groups have markedly incorporated the use of fashwave, as well as symbols that are typically connected to the accelerationist and neo-Nazi universe, such as the skullmask, the black sun, and the Celtic cross, among others. Some violent actions by neo-integralist groups – such as stealing antifascist banners and the aforementioned bombing of a comedy production company, as well as the nod to explicitly anti-Semitic discourse – have taken the place of a discourse that had previously been based almost exclusively on praising the myth of racial democracy and Christianity.

This is a continuous process of hybridization, whereby the traditional values of right-wing extremism in Brazil add to a rich global patchwork. Therefore, it is not solely about the importing of foreign values and expressions to the Brazilian context, but encompasses effectively building a sense of global appropriation and dialogue, wherein Brazilian exponents are active members and not mere recipients.

In addition to this process of "ideological impregnation," groups that adopt violent, armed, and virtually terrorist tactics (given their political nature) have been articulating in concrete ways. A testament to this is the articulation of Brazilian cells of international groups, such as the Misanthropic Division (between 2015 and 2020) and the Atomwafem Division (2021), in addition to the aforementioned Brazilian sect of the Hammerskins. These groups demonstrate that the manifestations of Brazilian neo-Nazism go beyond the initial model, based around skinheads, formal groups, or Holocaust denial that was the case during the emergence of "late neofascism."

Research endeavors that monitor these initiatives, such as the "Hate Map" (Mapa do Ódio) and the "Observatory of the Extreme Right" (Observatório da Extrema Direita), note the construction of a more complex, plural, internationalized, and violent scenario. It is even arguable that a third wave of neofascism has been forming in Brazil, one that could be characterized less by groups of varying sizes and more by the dissemination of violent actions perpetrated by individuals whose political identities rely on crimes, murders, and terrorist acts. This third wave would not be a separate, subsequent movement from the other two waves (1980–2000, 2000–2020), but would rather overlap with them, with the coexistence of different groups, trends, and tactics, with a greater impact on the actions of isolated individuals (lone wolves) and the establishment of digital environments as spaces for intellectual and political formation.

The challenge presented by the growth of the extreme right must be deemed not only a necessary object of analysis, but also a public security issue, given the highly incipient way in which Brazilian legislation discusses topics such as neo-Nazism, hate speech, Holocaust denialism, and the symbolism of the extreme right. This must also include discussions around the responsibility of so-called Big Techs and the effects of spreading this content against a backdrop of attacks on democracy.

Understanding the diversity of the neofascist movement in Brazil means analyzing this pendular movement between the local and the global, as well as informal spaces and the institutional and political field. For all intents and purposes, this is evidence that formal politics is not safe from neofascist attacks.

5 Considerations

The history of neofascism in Brazil is seen from the bottom up. By analyzing groups and leaders that have developed over the last few decades, it is noticeable that many agents have made the effort to turn neofascism into a concrete reference for the Brazilian far right. Despite its late nature compared to the rest of the world, Brazilian neofascism has succeeded in some of its collective endeavors, as it has been able to develop autonomy and establish a dialogue with other sectors of the radical and extreme right and international organizations.

The recent Brazilian political scene saw the emergence of the so-called "new rights," especially with the election of Bolsonaro, which helped to consolidate this movement. From the perspective of neofascism, the rise of this extreme-right leader to power was the first step toward legitimization and eventual participation in institutional politics. Furthermore, Bolsonarism's recurring nods to the violent acts of the Brazilian and international extreme right have naturalized messages – either encrypted or explicit – that include fascist references, especially Brazilian integralism and German national socialism.

Over two complementary phases, neofascism became more complex. It stopped being a space to reminisce about the 1930s and became a political asset, even if a marginal one. This warrants a warning. It is necessary to understand neofascism as a diverse, conflict-ridden environment capable of adapting to the most varied political conditions, from legislative mandates to terrorist tactics. On the one hand, this camp manages to promote more conservative discourses, with neo-integralist organizations, Bolsonarists, and neo-Pentecostal evangelicals sharing the motto "God, Homeland, Family." On the other hand, there have been cases based fundamentally on political violence, anti-Semitism, armamentism, and events such as attacks on schools that led to the death of dozens of adults, children, and teenagers. This is a sad new aspect of the Brazilian reality, which is a society traditionally marked by violence. From an analytical perspective, this phenomenon must be considered in its entirety. Its two strands are not separate because they are parts of different strategies within the same camp, essentially characterized by its constant radicalization.

Fascism, by definition, seeks holistic, palingenetic, and regenerative formats aimed at nations and societies it deems degenerate. Neo-fascists use similar arguments, but in a much more diverse network, and often through individual actions or small groups. Brazilian neofascism justifies this interpretation. Its smaller groups are, in fact, a novelty that exemplifies how neofascism can transform itself and endure. That decentralized form of neofascism that is not aimed at the masses is also a challenging object to analyze, given that it has built alternative networks of sociability and political action, which do not even rely on formal politics or visible initiatives. These are political identities formed through unusual means or even through spheres that have become common in our digital and everyday lives, especially among young adults and teenagers.

Therefore, it is of utmost importance to confront neofascism (and celebrations of fascism) as a challenge for our field of study, as well as for the democratic stability of countries with a long history of volatility, such as Brazil. After all, as can be understood from this Element (and as is corroborated by a well-established field of studies), the Brazilian extreme right has proved to be very politically capable over the last few years, and even a history written from the bottom up, like that of neofascism, is a testament to this.

References

Alcantara, S. R. (2015). Skinheads White Power na América do Sul: A internacionalização do discurso nacional-socialista da Blood & Honour. *Revista Espaço Acadêmico*, 15(175), pp. 18–26.

Almeida, A. (2004). *Skinheads: Os "mitos ordenadores" do Poder Branco paulista*. Master's dissertation (Mestrado em Ciências Sociais) – Programa de Pós-Graduação em Ciências Sociais. Pontifícia Universidade Católica de São Paulo.

Almeida, A. (2013). Divisão 18: A identidade de resistência de uma organização Skinhead White Power argentino-brasileira. *Revista Contemporâneos*, 1(11), pp. 1–21.

Bale, J. (2002). National Revolutionary Groupuscule and the Resurgence of Left-Wing Fascism: The Case of France's Nouvelle Résistance. *Patterns of Prejudice*, 36(3), pp. 25–45.

Bertonha, J. F. & Athaídes, R. (2023). *The Nazi Party and the German Communities Abroad: The Latin American Case*. London: Routledge.

Boisard, S. (2014). Pensando as direitas na América Latina objeto científico, sujeitos e temporalidades? *Varia Historia*, 30(52), pp. 85–100.

Bull, A. C. (2012). Neo-Fascism. In R. J. B. Bosworth, ed., *The Oxford Handbook of Fascism*. Oxford: Oxford University Press, pp. 586–605.

Caldeira Neto, O. (2017). A "direita envergonhada" e a fundação do Partido de Reedificação da Ordem Nacional. *Historiæ*, 7(2), pp. 79–102.

Caldeira Neto, O. (2019). "Adeus, Verde esperança!": Integralismo e a morte de Plínio Salgado. *Locus: Revista De História*, 25(1), pp. 1–19.

Carneiro, M. R. da S. R. (2012). Uma velha novidade: O integralismo no século XXI. *Boletim do Tempo Presente*, 3, pp. 1–26.

Chirio, M. (2018). *Politics in Uniform: Military Officers and Dictatorship in Brazil, 1960–1980*. Pittsburgh: University of Pittsburgh Press.

Copsey, N. (2020). Neo-Fascism: A Footnote to the Fascist Epoch? In C. Iordachi and A. Kallis, eds., *Beyond the Fascist Century*. London: Palgrave Macmillan, pp. 102–121.

Costa, M. R. (2000). *Os Carecas do Subúrbio: caminhos de um nomadismo moderno*. São Paulo: MUSA.

Costa Pinto, A. (2019). *Latin American Dictatorships in the Era of Fascism: The Corporatist Wave*. London: Routledge.

Dreifuss, R. (1989). *O jogo da Direita*. Rio de Janeiro: Editora Vozes.

Farias, J. A. (2023). A Extrema-Direita explosiva: Anticomunismo e atentados na distensão da Ditadura Civil-Milita. *Locus: Revista De História*, 28(2), pp. 351–375.

Finchelstein, F. (2019). *Do fascismo ao populismo na história*. São Paulo: Almedina.

Gonçalves, L. P. (2014). The Integralism of Plínio Salgado: Luso-Brazilian Relations. *Portuguese Studies*, 30(1), pp. 67–93.

Gonçalves, L. P. & Caldeira Neto, O. (2016). Brazilian Integralism and the Corporatist Intellectual Triad. *Portuguese Studies*, 32(2), pp. 225–243. https://doi.org/10.5699/portstudies.32.2.0225.

Gonçalves, L. P. & Caldeira Neto, O. (2022). *Fascism in Brazil: From Integralism to Bolsonarismo*. London: Routledge.

Griffin, R. (2003). From Slime Mould to Rhizome: An Introduction to the Groupuscular Right. *Patterns of Prejudice*, 37(1), pp. 27–50.

Griffin, R. (1991). *The Nature of Fascism*. London: Pinter Press.

Mammone, A. (2001). Revitalizing and De-Territorializing Fascism in the 1950s: The Extreme Right in France and Italy, and the Pan-National ("European") Imaginary. *Patterns of Prejudice*, 45(4), pp. 29–318.

Marchi, R. (2015). A identidade de Portugal no discurso da direita radical: do multirracialismo ao etnonacionalismo. *Estudos Ibero-Americanos*, 41(2), pp. 422–442.

Motta, R. P. S. (2020). *On Guard Against the Red Menace: Anti-Communism in Brazil, 1917–1964*. Liverpool: Liverpool University Press.

Mudde, C. (2019). *The Far Right Today*. Cambridge: Polity Press.

Napolitano, M. (2018). The Brazilian Military Regime, 1964–1985. *Oxford Research Encyclopedia of Latin American History*.

Pierucci, A. F. (1987). As bases da nova direita. *Novos Estudos Cebrap*, iss. 19.

Pirro, A (2022). Far Right: The Significance of an Umbrella Concept. *Nations and Nationalism*, 29(1), pp. 1–12. https://doi.org/10.1111/nana.12860.

Power, T. J. (2000). *The Political Right in Postauthoritarian Brazil: Elites, Institutions, and Democratization*. University Park: Pennsylvania State University Press.

Rodrigues, L. M. (1987). *Quem é quem na Constituinte: Uma análise sociopolítica dos partidos e deputados*. São Paulo: OESP-Maltese.

Santos, E. H. de J. (2022). Ativismo e extrema-direita no meio militar: Tensões e discursos que antecedem o bolsonarismo (1984–1998). *Brasiliana: Journal for Brazilian Studies*, 10(2). https://doi.org/10.25160/bjbs.v10i2.128414.

Shigunov, G. H. (2021). "Nossa Guerra contra vocês": Identitarismo e o caso da Legião Identitária. *Anais: IV Seminário Internacional História do Tempo Presente*, Florianópolis, pp. 1–15.

Traverso, E. (2018). *Las nuevas caras de la derecha*. Buenos Aires: Siglo XXI.

Valdez, R. S. (2024). Um nacionalismo transnacional? Estudo de caso da Nova Resistência, organização neofascista brasileira. Dissertation (Mestrado em Sociologia), Universidade Federal do Rio Grande do Sul.

Vasconcelos, F. T. R. (2023). A dissidência tradicionalista: A reinvenção da extrema direita brasileira como aliança "vermelho-marrom." *Almanaque de Ciência Política*, 7(2), pp. 1–29.

Von Beyme, K. (1988). Right-Wing Extremism in Post-War Europe. *West European Politics*, 11(2), pp. 1–18.

Zúquete, J. P. (2018). *The Identitarians: The Movement Against Globalism and Islam in Europe*. Notre Dame: University of Notre Dame Press.

Cambridge Elements

The History and Politics of Fascism

About the Series

Cambridge Elements in the History and Politics of Fascism is a series that provides a platform for cutting-edge comparative research in the field of fascism studies. With a broad theoretical, empirical, geographic, and temporal scope, it will cover all regions of the world, and most importantly, search for new and innovative perspectives.

Cambridge Elements ☰

The History and Politics of Fascism

Elements in the Series

Populism and Fascism
Carlos de la Torre

The Rise of Mass Parties, Liberal Italy, and the Fascist Dawn (1919–1924)
Goffredo Adinolfi

Neofascism and the Far Right in Brazil
Odilon Caldeira Neto

A full series listing is available at: www.cambridge.org/CEHF

For EU product safety concerns, contact us at Calle de José Abascal, 56–1°,
28003 Madrid, Spain or eugpsr@cambridge.org.

www.ingramcontent.com/pod-product-compliance
Ingram Content Group UK Ltd.
Pitfield, Milton Keynes, MK11 3LW, UK
UKHW022143080726
473066UK00010B/722

* 9 7 8 1 0 0 9 5 3 5 5 0 2 *